HOW TO
INVEST IN DEBT

HOW TO INVEST IN DEBT

A Complete Guide to
Alternative Opportunities

MICHAEL PELLEGRINO

Skyhorse Publishing

Skyhorse Publishing books may be purchased in bulk at special discounts for sales promotion, corporate gifts, fund-raising, or educational purposes. Special editions can also be created to specifications. For details, contact the Special Sales Department, Skyhorse Publishing, 307 West 36th Street, 11th Floor, New York, NY 10018 or info@ skyhorsepublishing.com.

Skyhorse® and Skyhorse Publishing® are registered trademarks of Skyhorse Publishing, Inc.®, a Delaware corporation.

Visit our website at www.skyhorsepublishing.com.

10 9 8 7 6 5 4 3 2

Library of Congress Cataloging-in-Publication Data is available on file.

Cover design by Rain Saukas
Cover photo credit: iStock Photo

Print ISBN: 978-1-5107-1519-6
Ebook ISBN: 978-1-5107-1521-9

Printed in the United States of America

Disclaimer

Dedication & Acknowledgment

This book is dedicated to my parents, Gerald and Maureen, who taught me to read and write and who paid for my education. I also thank my wife, Jennifer, and our children for patiently listening to me ramble on and on about investment concepts all the time.

Much thanks goes to my daughter, Jessica, who helped me to draft some of the more complex concepts.

Contents

Introduction

Debt Is Rampant—Let's Make Money

O ur "Debtor Nation" is facing a real problem with excessive debt. As of the end of 2016, the official debt of the United States government was $19.3 trillion, which breaks down as:

- $59,508 for every person living in the United States
- $154,407 for every household
- 106 percent of the US gross domestic product
- 553 percent of annual federal revenues.

It took decades to get ourselves into this situation, which will not go away any time soon. I have yet to hear of any politician with a concrete plan to address the debt crisis. Most won't even mention it. There is nothing that we can do as individuals to solve this problem, so, as private investors, we seek ways to profit from this situation. This book will introduce you to ten opportunities to invest in debt. These investments are not widely known or promoted. They are often purchased at deep discounts, and the debt is often secured by valuable real property. Our leaders in Washington, DC, have loaded us down with lemons, so let's learn how to make a profitable lemonade stand.

Through my twenty-five-year law practice, I have represented a variety of large and small investors who have profited from investing in various forms of debt. I have learned the advantages and disadvantages of each option, and I distilled a guide for ten ways to invest in debt, either directly or indirectly. These investment vehicles are unusual. They can provide a valuable hedge against stocks and bonds, which move with the economy. These alternative debt investments often perform better when the economy is struggling—contra other investments.

Most people have not even heard of these opportunities. There are very few books on these subjects, and they are not typically discussed on televised investment programs.

- Tax Liens
- Peer-to-Peer Loans through internet sites
- Defaulted Credit Card Debt at a Discount
- Defaulted Mortgage Notes
- Performing Mortgage Notes at a Discount
- Sheriff's Sales
- "White Knight" Rescues of Preforeclosure Properties
- Buying Foreclosed Properties
- Life Settlements & Viaticals
- Mortgage-Backed Securities

Each chapter in this book will introduce you to a different way to invest in debt. I'll explain how each investment vehicle works and tell you everything you need to know to participate in these opportunities. This book is not intended to promote these investments. I'm not selling any consulting services or webinars. I will lay out both the good and bad aspects of each concept and leave it up to you to decide which are for you.

Is This Stuff For You?

Some of these investment opportunities are not for everyone. They work well for a certain type of person with an entrepreneurial spirit, a stomach for risk, and a high level of self-motivation. In my experience, the most successful investors in these vehicles have run their own small business or have experience investing in real estate. Others may very well succeed with no real estate or small-business experience, but be honest with yourself. If you have always been a "nine-to-five" employee, and never got around to investing in real estate or even picking your own stocks, then the more complex investments may not be the place to start. Don't worry, we will also cover a few debt investments that don't require any specialized knowledge or work at all, such as peer-to-peer lending, mortgage-backed securities, and life settlements. There is something for everyone.

This book does not promote any "miracle" investments or "easy money." Some of the investment opportunities discussed are more like small businesses themselves than simple investments. In order to generate returns that are higher than average, an investor must find a way to gain separation from other investors. To beat the general market, an investor must gain an advantage over other investors and over the market itself by adding one or more these factors:

✓ Luck
✓ Risk
✓ Work
✓ Specialized knowledge or ability

Anyone can get "lucky" and pick a winning stock once in a while, but luck is not consistent, and you can't do anything to improve or manage your luck. In order to obtain consistent higher returns, investors gain an advantage through hard work and by developing an advanced knowledge and ability to manage risk. For example, anyone can hit a lucky basketball or golf shot once in a while, but if you want to consistently win at basketball or golf, you can't rely on lucky shots. This common-sense rule applies to investing as well, so if you want to consistently win financially, then you must put in the work and gain a specialized knowledge and skill that most others don't have. Learn to recognize opportunities that others don't see.

Risk and reward go hand in hand. Investments with high potential rewards always carry higher risks. You must be willing to take risks and also be capable of assessing and managing those risks.

But don't worry, there is a book that guides you through these markets — and you are already reading it! If you are with me so far, then you have what it takes to succeed. Keep reading for the information and skills that you need to set yourself apart, manage the inherent risks, and succeed with these investments.

Market Theory

In each chapter, I include a brief discussion of the theory as to why these investments can produce above-average returns. I know that "market theory" sounds a bit boring or complex, but a brief explanation helps to understand each investment vehicle, and why it might work for you. I'll keep it short!

The investments addressed in this book have varying pros and cons, but they all relate to debt, and they all take advantage of being part of "imperfect markets." By using the term "imperfect," I don't mean to imply that they are not good investments.

These investments have qualities that are far from what is considered to be "Perfect Market Competition," and because of those "imperfect market" qualities, it is possible to gain advantages and earn high profits.

"Perfect market competition" is purely theoretical. No market is truly perfect, but the theory is useful in comparing different markets. When a market is closer to being "perfect," it is harder to achieve outstanding returns. Markets that are further from "perfect" can generate higher returns because the imperfect aspects of the market create opportunities. What makes a market more or less perfect?

"Perfect Market" Factors:

1. *Liquidity*—Many buyers and sellers transacting on a constant basis;
2. *Non-Monopoly*—Many small competitors so that no one can dominate the market;
3. *Information*—Complete information is easily available to everyone about the product being sold and the prices paid by others; and
4. *Easy Access*—No barriers to entry into the market such as licensing, specialized knowledge, or large capital requirements.

Again, no market is truly "perfect," but the US stock market is an example of a market that is set up to score very high on these factors:

"Perfect Market" Factors as Applied to the US Stock Market:

1. *Liquidity*—Shares in most large companies are traded ***thousands*** of times each day. There are almost always buyers to match with sellers, so anyone can buy or sell any share in literally seconds.
2. *Non-Monopoly*—There are millions of buyers and sellers, and dozens of brokers to trade through;
3. *Information*—Information about publicly traded stocks is regulated and shared openly (despite examples of people who "cheat" with inside information). The stock markets are designed so that all investors have easy access to information about publicly traded companies, and instant knowledge of exactly what each stock is trading at on a moment-by-moment basis; and
4. *Easy Access*—Anyone over the age of 18 can open a brokerage account with as little as a few hundred dollars and begin to buy and sell stocks from a home computer or phone. No licensing, training, or specialized knowledge is required.

Because of these factors, which are designed to create transparency, fairness, and access, most people find it very difficult to consistently gain outlying results buying stocks. Even highly paid professional fund managers rarely beat the overall market on a consistent basis.

A basic understanding of this "perfect market" theory is helpful in understanding why the investments discussed in this book can create exceptional results in very "imperfect" markets. Let's take tax liens as an example. We haven't gotten to the chapter on tax liens yet, so don't worry if you aren't familiar with them yet; but let's run them through the "perfect market" factors as a way to further illustrate how these factors work:

"Perfect Market" Factors as Applied to Tax Liens:

1. *Liquidity*—Unlike stocks and bonds, tax liens are not sold through a broker. They are generally sold at public auctions in the county or municipality where the property is located. There is no generally accepted secondary market to sell a lien. So if an investor wants to "cash out," he or she must go out and find a buyer;

2. *Non-Monopoly*—There are many tax lien investors, so the public auctions can be competitive; but sellers are generally limited to municipalities or counties, so there is a firm limit on when and where an investor can buy a tax lien;

3. *Information*—Some critical information is readily available for tax lien investors such as tax-assessed property value, and photos are often available on line; but there is no public record of prior trades (which stock investors rely upon), and a tax lien investor is not permitted to enter or inspect the subject property, so investors are expected to bid with very limited information; and

4. *Easy Access*—Anyone over the age of 18 can buy tax liens, but most sales are live auctions, so an investor must either travel to attend the auctions or train and pay a bidder to attend an auction. Training and some degree of specialized knowledge is needed.

This comparison of the tax liens market to the stock market demonstrates how the tax lien market is far from a "perfect market."

So why is an imperfect market a better place to invest? Good question. It isn't necessarily a better investment for every investor. If you seek a safe and secure investment in which you will get the same returns as the general market, then you should invest in bank CDs or index funds. There is nothing wrong with that safe and secure approach.

But imperfections or inefficiencies in a market can drastically reduce competition and can create opportunities for a sharp investor to buy at a deeply discounted price—a "bargain." If you seek to "beat the market" and shoot for some outlying gains, then look for imperfect markets.

For example, if an investor is seeking to buy a two-family house in a particular county, that buyer would have access to photos, recent comparable sales, and other detailed information listed on the Multiple Listing Service ("MLS") website. The buyer could walk through and inspect the house. All other potential buyers have the same information at the tips of their fingers, so it is not reasonable to expect to get a great bargain. By definition, the buyer must be willing to pay more than anyone else is willing to offer at that given time. That system is fine if the goal is to reach a fair price. An investor seeking a true bargain, however, is unlikely to find it on the MLS. A bargain hunter must look in "imperfect markets" to find truly undervalued assets. That is what this book is about.

Most people who invest in the vehicles discussed in this book also hold traditional stocks and bonds. The options in this book merely present an alternative for a portion of a well-balanced investment portfolio. These debt investment opportunities do not typically move up or down with the stock and bond markets. Some tend to perform even better in a bad economy. Personally, I consider these to be a useful hedge against my other more traditional investments, and a way to swing for larger results on a small portion of my funds.

So Why Haven't I Heard of This?

I've heard this question many times. *If these investments are so attractive, why haven't I heard of them? Why hasn't my broker or financial advisor told me about them?* Most people who bought this book probably have at least heard about tax liens or sheriff's sales, but it is true that most of the subjects are not common knowledge, and the reason is fairly simple.

- ✓ *No commissions.* Most of these investments do not generate a commission or fee, so brokers and financial advisors don't bother with them. Why should they develop a specialty in an area that does not earn them a fee?
- ✓ *Specialized knowledge and experience.* These investments are not meant for everyone. As detailed in each chapter, these opportunities are not for rookies. Many require a large cash investment, others are restricted to qualified investors with a high net worth and income level. Most of these investments also require some degree of experience, work, and knowledge.

Know the Terms

As unusual terms are introduced in each chapter, I'll provide definitions that are relevant for the subject matter of that that chapter. These basic terms are more common and relevant to all of the subjects:

Secured loan: A loan that is secured by assets such as real property, accounts receivable, or any other item of value. If the debtor fails to repay the loan, the creditor can have the assets seized to satisfy the loan. For example, a mortgage loan is secured by real property, and the creditor may foreclose on the property if the loan is not repaid.

Bankruptcy: A court procedure that (in simplest terms) temporarily stops collection efforts and eliminates a debtor's obligation to pay (forgives) certain debts;

Collateral: Assets such as real property that are pledged or "collateralized" to secure a debt.

Creditor: A person or entity who is owed money.

Debtor: A person or entity who owes money.

Equity: The amount of money that a property is worth in excess of any liens on that property.

Foreclose: The legal procedure that a creditor uses to seize real property that a debtor has pledged as security for a loan.

Lien: A legal instrument that is recorded to secure repayment of debt by imposing a legal claim on collateral such as real property. If the debt is not repaid as required, the creditor may enforce the lien by foreclosing or seizing the collateral.

Note: A legal document that memorializes a promise to repay debt in accordance with certain recited terms such as interest and a repayment date.

Priority: The order in which liens may be enforced against secured property.

Redeem: To pay off a tax lien or other type of debt. Sometimes referred to as a "redemption."

Security: An asset such as real property that secures the repayment of a loan.

Sheriff's Sale: A court-ordered sale of real property that was pledged as collateral to secure a loan. The sale proceeds are used to satisfy the loan.

Qualified / Accredited Investor: Having an annual income of at least $200,000 ($300,000 for joint income) or a net worth of at least $1 million.

Chapter Format:

For the sake of clarity and continuity, each chapter is structured in a similar way. Some of the subject matter overlaps and applies to other investment vehicles, so the repeating format may be helpful in understanding and comparing the different investment options. Each chapter includes a discussion of the following factors so you can easily compare and contrast the characteristics of each investment:

1. Overview of Investment
2. Words of Wisdom from an Experienced Investor
3. Minimum Capital Requirement
4. Scalability
5. Liquidity—Cash Flow and Resale Market.
6. Priority over Other Forms of Debt
7. A Little on Market Theory
8. What Can Go Wrong? Common Pitfalls
9. Common Terms
10. Source Books, Consultants, Websites and Sellers

You have already taken the first steps of picking up this book and starting to read it, so you are on the right track to exploring these relatively unknown investment concepts. I hope the chapters that follow lead you to new avenues to achieve your financial goals.

1

Tax Liens & Tax Deeds
Make Money by Paying Other People's Taxes

Income tax, sales tax, real estate tax . . . everyone hates to pay taxes, but most people don't know that there is a way to make great profit from paying taxes. This chapter will tell you how to invest in high-yield property tax liens that are secured by first-priority liens on real estate.

High interest and low risk are very attractive terms these days. With interest rates near historic lows and the high volatility of the stock market, many people have been drawn to alternative investments. Tax liens accrue interest at 21 percent or higher, they're secured by a first-priority lien on property chosen by the investor, and they offer the added bonus of possibly of obtaining ownership of the property at a big discount.

Summary Points

1. **Specialized Knowledge:** Real estate valuation & rehab
2. **Minimum Capital Requirement:** $5,000
3. **Scalability:** Yes
4. **Liquidity:** Limited; resale of tax liens is not well organized
5. **Priority over other forms of debt:** Highest
6. **Barriers to Entry:** None

My law practice has been focused on representing tax lien investors in New Jersey for over twenty years. I've written a law review article and a book on New Jersey tax liens, and I have been a speaker at the New Jersey Bar Association's continuing legal education annual seminar for over ten years. I'd say that I know more about tax liens than any other subject. I'll outline the positive and negative aspects, and I'll leave it to you to decide whether this unique investment vehicle is right for you.

Unfortunately, each state has a different statutory scheme covering how tax liens are to be sold and foreclosed. This chapter will provide an overview of the various jurisdictions. There are a lot of details, and it would not be possible to cover each state in this chapter. Like all of the other chapters, I have included a list of some books on investing in tax liens. This subject is far more complex than what can be covered in this chapter, so you will find these books to provide a more detailed and complete review. There is no substitute for good old-fashioned personal experience and one-on-one communication. If any questions remain, call your local tax lien attorney!

How Does This Work?

Like most things in life, there is a short, simple story and a long, detailed story. Property tax liens can be summarized in a very simple paragraph, or it could take years of experience and an entire book. The short and simple version is as follows:

> **Tax liens are sold by tax collectors to make up for unpaid property taxes. Local governments (like counties and municipalities) depend on the collection of property taxes and other assessments to pay for services provided to residents. Local governments could not operate without the consistent collection of these funds, so it creates a problem when property owners fail to pay their property taxes. In exchange for the payment of overdue property taxes, an investor is issued a tax lien that generates interest until redeemed (paid off) by the property owner or another interested person. The tax certificate represents a high-priority lien on a delinquent tax payer's property. If the lien is not redeemed within a period of time, the lien holder may foreclose and obtain clean title to the underlying property. Tax lien investors make money by collecting interest on liens that are redeemed, and by foreclosing on properties and reselling them.**

That's the short version. For the long version, you will have to read the rest of this chapter.

Who Should Invest in Tax Liens?

Tax liens offer a compelling investment vehicle. Investors get a high priority lien at a high interest rate on real property selected by the investor. To top it off, the investor may gain ownership of the underlying real estate for a cost far less than the property is worth. That's the attractive side of this investment. That's why there are so many people interested in buying tax liens, and it's probably why you are reading this.

Before we get into details, let's address specifically what a tax lien is. A "lien" is a legal restriction on property rights to secure repayment of debt. A tax lien is represented by a piece of paper known as a Tax Sale Certificate, which is recorded in the county records along with other liens on real property such as mortgages. The lien stays on the property until it is "redeemed" or paid off. The owner of the property still maintains control over, and responsibility for, the property, but the property generally cannot be sold or refinanced without paying off the lien. If the lien is not redeemed, it can be foreclosed, and the tax lien holder may become the new owner of the property, free and clear of any other liens.

That phrase "free and clear of any other liens" is very important. This means that if you foreclose on a tax lien, you can wipe out any mortgage, judgments, or any other liens, and you will become the owner of the property with clean title—with a few exceptions as determined by State laws (for example, newer—"subsequent"—tax liens) that generally have priority over older ("prior") tax liens, so they are an exception to the priority rule. In some states, you will obtain free and clear title at the conclusion of the tax lien foreclosure, but in other states, you must file an additional "quiet title" suit to obtain clean title.

Why This Works

Tax liens are an option for adding diversity to a balanced investment portfolio. Unlike other investments, the value of a tax lien is not affected by the economy, the stock market, or interest rate fluctuations. A tax lien's value is based solely on the taxes that have been paid by the investor and the applicable interest rate. No outside economic factors can change that. Of course, if a tax lien is foreclosed, then the real estate market will determine the value of the investment, but most tax liens are eventually redeemed, and the real estate market generally does not fluctuate greatly.

Most investments are judged by six common factors: income, growth potential, safety of investment capital, liquidity, diversification, and simplicity. Tax liens compare well under the standard benchmarks:

1. **Income** . . . . **Very Good**
   Tax liens accrue an exceptionally high interest rate.

2. **Growth potential** . . . . **Fair**
   Tax liens provide an opportunity to obtain property for less than its value, but such opportunities are rare.

3. **Safety of investment capital** . . . . . . **Very Good**
   Tax liens are secured by a first priority lien on real estate, so it is very likely that your investment will be returned.

4. **Liquidity** . . . . **Bad**
   There is no organized secondary market, so it can be difficult to cash out of a tax lien.

5. **Diversification** . . . . **Very Good**
   There is no correlation to other investment markets.

6. **Simplicity** . . . . **Bad**
   Investing in tax liens requires more time and experience than most other investments.

Of course, *everything* has its downside. Investing in tax liens is certainly not without risk and hard work. Unlike passive investments such as stocks, bonds, and certificates of deposit, buying tax liens is closer to a business than an investment. This takes time and some knowledge. To be successful, investors need to develop an ability to evaluate the condition of properties and assess their value. Many people just don't have the time or energy to devote to this type of undertaking. For them, publicly traded securities are the extent of their investment portfolio, and there is certainly nothing wrong with that. If you do not have extra time to devote to this venture, don't buy tax liens.

Another important consideration before you buy your first tax lien is the long-term commitment that is required. There is no efficient secondary market for tax liens, so there is no simple and efficient way to trade out of a lien if the need arises. With stocks and bonds, on the other hand, the investor can call a broker at any time and simply sell the investment for its current value less the cost of the broker's commission. Even bank CDs can be cashed in either at the end of the term or at any time with the payment of a penalty. The holder of a tax lien must go out and find someone willing to buy the lien, and then negotiate a price—which of course may be more or less than the redemption value of the lien.

Aside from the term of this commitment, investors must also make further financial commitments to a lien after it is purchased. Unlike most other investments that require only one, up-front payment, purchasing a tax lien is a long-term commitment requiring additional payments each year for at least three years. One of my friends who has been investing in tax liens for a long time likens the initial purchase of a tax lien to the initial ante in a poker game. Buying the tax lien just gets you started, like tossing that first chip onto the poker table. In order to maintain the priority of the lien, and to accrue more interest, lien holders must continue to pay subsequent taxes each year. If the lien is not paid off after a few years, the tax lien holder will also have to fund the costs and fees involved in foreclosure proceedings.

Another unusual negative aspect of this investment vehicle is that investors do not have control over what liens they can buy. If someone wants to invest in a particular stock or bond, there is no question that he or she will succeed with a simple phone call to a broker. Tax liens are different in that each is unique. Each tax lien is a legal interest in a unique piece of real estate, so each lien is as unique as the underlying property.

For the last several years, there has been fierce competition among bidders at tax lien auctions. Many investors often get shut out at the auction, having been outbid by more aggressive investors. Sometimes all of the time spent looking at properties and reviewing public records can be for nothing.

Finally, as addressed in more detail later in this chapter, tax lien investors will eventually face the morality issues connected with foreclosing on a family's home or evicting elderly widows! Before you buy your first tax lien, you should be aware of the emotional and moral aspects of this investment.

The purpose of addressing these negative aspects of tax lien investing is not to discourage people from buying tax liens. *(I make my living representing tax lien investors!)* I simply want investors to be aware of what they are getting into. I've had far too many inexperienced investors come to my law offices with problems that could have been avoided had they simply known all of the risks, or if they had at least known which questions to ask. Most other sources of information about tax lien investing either completely ignore these negative aspects or gloss over them.

Despite the negatives, I know of no other investment vehicle that can generate such a high rate of interest secured by real estate at a low lien-to-value ratio. This high security and rate of return, coupled with the possibility of acquiring real estate worth far more than you invested, makes tax liens a valuable addition to an investment portfolio.

Now that we have gotten most of the negative aspects out of the way, we can get into the details about how to buy tax liens.

Tax Liens vs Tax Deeds

Some states sell "tax deeds" instead of tax liens. Tax deeds (like tax liens) are sold to the public to convert tax delinquencies into cash flow for the local government. The basic concepts are similar, but the key difference is whether the investor acquires a *tax lien* or a *tax deed*. In most states, the property owner has a period of time to pay off the tax delinquency and retain the property.

Tax Lien States

Alabama, Arizona, Colorado, Connecticut, Florida, Illinois, Indiana, Iowa, Kentucky, Louisiana, Maryland, Massachusetts, Mississippi, Missouri, Montana, Nebraska, New Jersey, New York, Ohio, Rhode Island, South Dakota, Vermont, West Virginia, Wyoming.

In my home state of New Jersey, and other tax lien states, investors bid on and purchase "tax lien certificates." You are not acquiring an ownership interest in the property; rather, you are paying the taxes and acquiring a lien on the property. The owner of the property must pay off the amount of the lien plus interest and penalties in order to have the lien removed. If the lien is not "redeemed" (paid) within a specified "redemption period," the purchaser of the tax lien certificate may foreclose on the property. Each state has different rules and laws controlling when and how tax liens may be foreclosed. In some states, the tax lien will expire if it is not foreclosed within the time allowed.

How Tax Liens Are Purchased

Each state has different laws that specify interest rates, redemption periods, and bidding procedures. Tax liens are not sold like other, more common investments. There are no listings in the financial pages of your newspaper, and you cannot just call your broker as you would to buy a stock, bond, or commodity. There are no sales commissions, no monthly statements in the mailbox, and generally no salesmen or advisors. This takes a little more work, but it can be worth the effort.

Auction Process

Tax lien auctions are the primary way that tax liens are purchased. They are usually well attended and can get very exciting. The auction process is always confusing to newcomers, so it is advisable to attend a few auctions before you begin bidding. This will give you a feel for the process, and you may get pointers from some of the more experienced bidders. Tax lien auctions are generally held once per year in each municipality or county, so it may be impossible to personally attend every auction that you'd like. This is becoming less of an issue, because more and more auctions are being held online through services such as "RealAuction" and "Grant Street." This change to online bidding is rapidly gaining popularity and is more efficient than live, in-person auctions, but the ease and efficiency of the online auctions creates even more competition for investors.

Prior to a tax sale auction, the tax collector is required to create a tax sale list that identifies each property that will be subject to tax sale. The list includes a legal property description and the amount due on the lien. Investors watch the legal advertisements in local newspapers to learn of upcoming sales, or they pay clipping services that provide notice of each published auction. There are also a few websites that, for a fee, provide information on all upcoming sales and include lists of the liens that will be sold. Unfortunately, the lists that are advertised and posted on websites are typically reduced by the time that auction occurs because many liens are paid off. It is common for up to one-third of the list to be paid off before the auction, so much of your time is wasted on presale due diligence, evaluating properties that are removed from the list before the sale begins.

Tax sale auctions are conducted under different rules depending upon which state you are in. In New Jersey, for example, investors do not bid on the **_price_** of the tax lien. They bid on the **_interest rate_** that will accrue on the money that they pay to buy the lien. The successful bidder is required to pay the outstanding property taxes with interest and penalties as of that date. The auction for each lien is won by the investor who bids the lowest interest rate.

In other states, a random "round robin" selection process is used so each investor has an equal chance without competitively bidding against one another.

Still in other states, tax sales are conducted in the typical auction process where the winner is simply determined by who bids the highest amount of money.

No Collusion or Bid-Rigging

It is illegal for bidders to make any agreements or deals to reduce or interfere with competition at the auctions. This is known as collusion or bid-rigging. Don't do it.

Bidders are usually required to register before bidding at a sale. A few states even require a deposit, usually in certified funds, in order to register. For most lien sales, payment is expected in full, in certified funds, at the conclusion of the sale. A few states will allow time to go to the bank and secure funds, but some will not let you leave without paying. If you do not pay within the allotted time frame, the lien will be resold.

Recording

Regardless of which method is used to buy a tax lien or tax deed, it must be recorded in order to put the public on notice of the existence and ownership of the lien. All tax liens and assignments of liens must be recorded in the county records in the county where the property is located. Of course, each county clerk's office charges a recording fee. A tax lien cannot be foreclosed unless the lien is recorded.

Tax Deeds, States

Some jurisdictions sell "tax deeds" instead of tax liens. These states include:

> Alaska, Arizona, Arkansas, California, Connecticut, Delaware, Florida, Geor-gia, Hawaii, Idaho, Indiana, Kansas, Maine, Massachusetts, Michigan, Min-nesota, Montana, Nevada, New York, North Carolina, North Dakota, Ohio, Oklahoma, Oregon, Pennsylvania, South Carolina, Tennessee, Texas, Utah, Virginia, Washington, West Virginia, Wisconsin.

Tax deeds vary slightly by state, but in general, investors acquire a ***deed*** to the subject property, rather than just a ***lien*** on the property. Some states sell "***redeemable*** tax deeds," and others sell "***nonredeemable*** tax deeds." This is a critical distinction. If you buy a *redeemable* tax deed, then the property owner has a certain period of time to pay off the delinquent taxes, known as a "redemption period." If the taxes are not paid off within the redemption period, then the delinquent taxpayer loses the property. Redeemable tax deeds have redemption periods and interest rates or penalties similar to tax liens, and at the expiration of the redemption period, the investor must com-plete an administrative or legal process to obtain clear marketable title. If the property owner wishes to pay off the delinquent taxes before a deadline set by the local county or state, then he or she must pay the amount of the delinquent tax, plus interest. The property owner does not have to pay the premium or overbid, but the owner must pay interest on the entire bid (including the premium). The premium will be refunded by the county to the bidder.

If the property owner does not pay off the delinquent taxes before the deadline set by the local county or state, then the investor becomes the owner of the property by virtue of the tax deed, the former owner moves out, and the "premium" or "overbid" funds can be claimed by the former owner or junior lien holders in accordance with local priority laws—the highest priority gets paid first.

If you buy a *nonredeemable* tax deed, on the other hand, there is no redemption period. The deed is treated like any other deed, and the investor has acquired full ownership at the time of the sale. This is the simplest method of tax sale, similar to a sale at the end of a mortgage foreclosure.

One of the major differences relates to the investor's liability. Tax deeds carry some liabilities associated with owning property, even though the ownership is subject to possible redemption. The tax deed holder may be held liable for code violations or any other liability associated with property ownership. An investor who holds a tax lien, on the other hand, has no liability for the property unless and until the lien is foreclosed. If the property turns out to be worthless or undesirable, the tax lien holder may just walk away from the lien without foreclosing, with no liability.

It's not that easy with a tax deed. If you purchase a worthless piece of property, you're stuck with the property and the accompanying tax bills. In some states you may also be liable for other liens on the property if you purchase the deed at a tax sale. Some states may have different types of sales: one in which all liens are conveyed with the deed, and one in which properties are sold free and clear of other liens. You need to check this out before you bid on property at a tax deed sale. In most states, the deed that is issued is without any warranty as to the title of the property. This means that you may have to perfect the title on the property before you can sell it to someone else. This is commonly known as a "quiet title action," and you'll need an attorney to handle it for you.

Bidding at tax deed sales is a little different from at most lien sales. At tax deed sales the "premium bid" or "overbidding" method is used. Bidding in most tax deed states is based on the value of the property, as opposed to the interest rate or tax delinquency. For example, in some states, like South Carolina, tax deeds are regularly bid up as high as 70 percent of the value of the property. Bidding procedures in "tax deed states" varies widely. Some states will start the bidding at the amount of delinquent taxes plus penalties and interest; other states start the bidding at the assessed amount of the property. Some states even start the opening bid at an amount lower than the delinquent taxes.

Picking the Right Liens and Tax Deeds

The first step in choosing the right lien is determining what your expectations are. If you are satisfied with accruing high interest, it is much easier to find suitable liens to purchase. If, on the other hand, you are seeking liens that are less likely to be redeemed so you can acquire the property through foreclosure, you will have to search much harder.

The primary factor here is that over 95 percent of all tax liens redeem. If it is inter-est income that you are after, you can hardly miss. Although it would be very foolish, you could blindly pick any lien, and the odds are overwhelmingly in your favor that the lien will eventually be paid off. Recognizing this, most tax lien investors buy liens with the *expectation* that they will redeem

On the most basic level, investors would rather buy liens on more attractive, valu-able properties. There is always the small chance that a lien will not be redeemed and you will become the owner of the property through foreclosure, so you would not want to buy a lien on any property that you would not want to eventually own.

Due Diligence

Before you even think of bidding at a tax lien auction or paying for an assignment of a lien, you have to do your due diligence. Research the underlying property to ensure that the lien is worth buying.

Although any investment in tax liens is secured by a high-priority lien on real property, your investment is only secured by the value of the underlying property. Usually this is not a problem because taxes are generally a very small percentage of the assessed value of the real estate. Nevertheless, experienced investors spend a substan-tial amount of time evaluating the underlying property for each tax lien they intend to purchase.

Because the redemption rate is more than 95 percent, investors may be inclined to overlook the issue of property value. This can be a fatal error because if a property has little or no value, the lien will not be redeemed, and you will be stuck owning a property with little or no value.

Property value is the best indicator of whether a lien will be redeemed. This is not rocket science: if the property has value, the lien is likely to be redeemed, and if the property has no value, the lien is very unlikely to be redeemed. The risk of this pitfall can only be eliminated through a careful appraisal of the underlying property.

As you would imagine, property owners are typically uninspired to allow entry onto their property or to share information with tax lien investors. Because tax lien investors have no right to enter and inspect the underlying properties, diligent analysis, with a lack of in-depth personal inspection, is difficult if not impossible.

A drive-by inspection and review of public records is typically the extent of analysis that can be done. Investors usually rely on public records such as tax assessment files, building department records, zoning and tax maps, and previous sale records that are available through municipal and county public records.

There are also due diligence services available for a fee. These services can be found on the Internet or by speaking with bidders at any tax sale.

Which Liens to Bid On

It makes sense for new investors to buy liens that are close to home. The advantages of investing in your own area are that you will have a better feel for property values, and it will be much easier to keep an eye on the properties after you have bought liens on them. Any significant changes in the condition and value of the property may affect your ongoing decision of whether to pay subsequent taxes and when to begin foreclosure. With the high competition for tax liens, you will inevitably find that you'll have to venture farther away in order to buy more and more liens, but buying close to home is a good way to start.

Some investors are only interested in acquiring real estate. Of course, they don't mind accruing high interest, but they have a clear focus on buying liens with the goal of foreclosing and getting the property. There is no single way to ensure that any given lien will not redeem, but there are some factors that reduce likelihood of redemption.

Their primary course is to buy liens that are already in the foreclosure process, so they can avoid the long holding period. These liens are hard to come by, but this type of investor typically contacts all of the larger institutional tax lien investors and inquires about the availability of such liens. It is common to pay a reasonable premium over the redemption value for liens that are close to the end of foreclosure proceedings. A premium payment is usually the only way to pry one of these liens loose. Keep in mind, however, that many liens redeem just before the foreclosure is completed. Any premium that is paid over redemption value for an assignment will be lost upon redemption.

Although there is no way to accurately predict whether a lien will be redeemed, you can imagine circumstances that lead to foreclosure of a property. You can ask yourself two questions:

Does it appear that no one has any interest in the property?
Generally liens on property owned by an estate or heirs of a deceased owner have a lower redemption rate. Liens on unoccupied houses (board-ups) and undeveloped land are also less likely to be redeemed.

Does it appear that the owner is financially troubled?
Properties that appear run-down and unmaintained are popular targets, and as you may expect, properties in less desirable neighborhoods and towns have

lower redemption rates. The existence of many other liens on a given property is also a strong indication that the lien will not be redeemed. If all of the liens add up to more than the property is worth, it is more likely that the foreclosure will be completed.

Paying Subsequent Taxes

Property taxes generally come due every three months, and of course, taxes continue to accrue even after a tax lien is sold. Property taxes that come due after the sale of a tax lien are referred to as "subsequent taxes" or "subs" because they arise subsequent to the purchase of a tax lien. One of the key aspects of investing in tax liens is to *grow your lien* by paying subsequent taxes ("subs") after you buy the lien. Tax lien holders are entitled to pay subsequent taxes on the property if the taxes are not paid by the owner of the property. There are two reasons why it is important to pay subs. First, it increases the amount of money invested that accrues interest. Second, it preserves the first-priority status of your lien.

Every time you pay subs on a tax lien, the redemption value of the tax lien is increased by the amount of subsequent taxes that you pay, and the subs always accrue interest. Each state has different rules for how subs accrue interest. In some states like New Jersey, subs always accrue interest at 18 percent! No auctions. No need for more research and due diligence. No extra work. You just pay the taxes as they become due, and you have the subs added to the value of your lien.

If you, as a tax lien holder, do not pay the subsequent taxes, then each quarter of unpaid subsequent taxes will become a lien that has priority over your lien. Eventually you will either have to pay it off, or you will be foreclosed.

Redemption: The Good/Bad News

The good news: You have a check coming!
The bad news: You are not going to own the property.

The overwhelming majority of tax liens are redeemed (paid off) before foreclosure is completed. In fact, most liens are paid off before foreclosure proceedings are even started. All tax lien investors know this, but hope springs eternal, and people can't help but get their hopes up. As the lien gets older and the redemption value keeps rising, the lien holder starts to think of scenarios under which the owner will let the property go to foreclosure.

As foreclosure proceedings get close to the end, my office often gets calls from anxious clients asking if we think this one will reach Final Judgment. It is human nature to hope for the best, and this is the exciting upside to this business. Since most tax liens are eventually redeemed, however, it is best not to anticipate getting the property.

In my experience foreclosing on hundreds of liens per year over the past ten years, I have found that about 80 percent of liens that go into foreclosure are paid off. The overall redemption percentage is much higher because many liens redeem before they even go into foreclosure. My larger clients advise me that over 98 percent of New Jersey tax liens redeem.

The bottom line? Try to focus on the positive. Take the redemption money and reinvest it in more liens.

Foreclosure

Most tax lien investors do not consider property acquisition to be their primary goal. The majority of tax liens purchased at auction redeem before foreclosure even begins. Each state imposes a "holding period" before foreclosure can be started. The holding period can be anywhere from three months to three years. This is primarily a game of accruing interest.

The fun and excitement, however, doesn't come from watching your interest churn. *Although that is a beautiful thing.* Investors get excited about the prospect of acquiring property for much less than market value by foreclosing. Most people don't stand around at a cocktail party bragging about their blended rate of interest, but you will hear tax lien investors reliving every detail of how they foreclosed on a property and made a killing. Some of my clients cannot resist calling me each and every time we get a final judgment on one of their files, to review how great the property is and how much profit they plan to make. It is a thrill.

Although taking property through foreclosure cannot be considered the *primary* goal of most investors due to the high redemption rate, it is the ***ultimate*** goal.

Selecting the Right Attorney

Having focused my law practice on tax liens for the past ten years, I may be biased, but I feel compelled to stress that choosing the right attorney is a very important factor in succeeding in this venture. Tax lien foreclosure is a highly specialized field in which the vast majority of lawyers have no experience.

Don't get me wrong, I am not saying that this is rocket science. It isn't an exceptionally difficult area of practice, but there are several factors that demand specialization.

The foreclosure process is technical in nature and must be done precisely in order for it to result in good marketable title. Many people proceed through the long foreclosure process and obtain a Final Judgment only to then discover that the foreclosure proceedings were fatally flawed, and worthless. The rules for locating and serving defendants must be followed exactly, and the pleadings must specify certain information exactly.

Tips from the Pros

I have worked with many investors for up to ten or even twenty years, so it was difficult to decide whom to invite to share a few pearls of wisdom.

T.J. Ryan has seen it all. He's worked with very large institutional investors and also consulted with small buyers.

> For small investors, local knowledge is the key to successful investing. Property values and neighborhood conditions change quickly from block to block. I love all of the new technology and available data on line, but it can give you a false sense about a particular property. There is no substitute for being personally familiar with the area in which you are investing. Living in Jersey City for almost 10 years and being involved in local real estate development has helped me make millions in profits from liens that other investors passed upon. I always advise new investors to start locally in areas that they know well. T.J. Ryan

My friend Joanne Musa is known online as the *Tax Lien Lady*, and she is a leading authority on tax lien investing throughout all of the states. She trains new investors and posts tons of information on her website, TaxLienLady.com and her free webinars. Her book *Tax Lien Investing Secrets* is a Best Seller on Amazon, and it is considered to be a must-read for anyone who is considering investing in this field.

Although Mike has done a great job summarizing this exciting opportunity, one chapter of a book can not possibly cover all that needs to be said. I've been investing in tax liens for almost 15 years in a few different states, and I've investigated how this works in most of the country and I'm still learning more about the nuances of how this works in different states all the time. State laws that govern tax sales keep changing. So I like to keep my finger on the pulse of the industry by investing in a couple of different states myself and talking to experts who are currently investing in other states around the country.

One of the points that I make to all of my subscribers and new students is that the vast majority of tax liens redeem. Tax lien investing is generally not a way to get property for "pennies on the dollar" as some would suggest. But it is a way to have your money working for you to earn a higher rate of interest than you could get in most traditional secured investments.

—Joanne Musa, TaxLienLady.com

What Can Go Wrong? Common Pitfalls

Tax liens are an attractive investment for many reasons. They offer a high interest rate, secured by a first-priority lien on property that the investor chooses. Plus, there is a chance that the investor may obtain title to the underlying real estate. As with everything else in life, though, there are a few pitfalls. Here is the stuff you won't find in any infomercial or national book.

All of the other books and infomercials promoting tax liens are directed toward the entire nation, and they are almost entirely devoid of any detail. Each state has different rules and procedures regarding the sale, redemption, and foreclosure of tax liens. Be aware of this problem and make sure that any source of information you consult is applicable in your state.

Some very smart people have lost significant amounts of money by relying on inaccurate information or by not even being aware of a risk that they were undertaking. One investor came to me after losing more than $10,000 on a tax lien that redeemed. He had bought the lien by private assignment from a more experienced tax lien investor, and he paid a large premium above the redemption value of the lien. He didn't realize that this premium would not be recovered if the lien was paid off. When the lien redeemed, he received $10,000 less than he had paid. There was nothing that could be done for him.

Another investor bought a tax lien by private assignment and lost more than $15,000 because the city was foreclosing on a subsequent tax lien that wiped his lien out. He was advised of the city's pending in rem foreclosure when he bought the lien, but he didn't pay off the city's lien in time because he was told that it would be no problem to pay off the city's lien even after the city's foreclosure was completed. Inaccurate information costs money. Final judgments are usually *final*.

Even the simple process of paying off subsequent tax liens can cost big bucks if the proper steps are not taken. A new tax lien investor came to my offices and explained that she had purchased a lien several years ago and had been paying the subsequent taxes diligently each quarter as they became due. We began the foreclosure proceedings, and, as with most liens, it was promptly redeemed. Only then did we discover that the lien holder had not been filing an Affidavit of Subsequent Tax Payment when she made each quarterly payment of subsequent taxes. The payments she had made over the years were not credited to her tax lien. They were simply accepted by the tax collector as an ordinary tax payment. She was understandably very upset and asked: "How was I supposed to know about this?" It is hard to ask questions when you don't even know what to ask.

The staff of most tax collectors' offices are generally helpful, but they are usually very busy, and they are not responsible for giving investment advice. Nevertheless, most tax lien investors have learned a lot from speaking with tax collectors who have been involved with the tax sale and redemption process for years.

Bankruptcy

The main point that all tax lien investors need to know is that tax liens are non dischargeable in bankruptcy. This means that tax liens remain in place during and after any bankruptcy proceeding.

Bankruptcy is a complicated area that is way beyond the scope of this book. My intention is only to introduce the reader to a few basic concepts. I strongly suggest that any tax lien holder consult with legal counsel if they get involved with a bankruptcy.

As soon as a property owner files a bankruptcy petition, an Automatic Stay is imposed, which stops anyone else from taking any action to collect debt or take property from the person who filed bankruptcy. This Automatic Stay, of course, applies to tax lien foreclosure. You will continue to accrue interest and your lien will retain its high priority, but you will not be able to begin or continue with foreclosure proceedings unless the bankruptcy court either dismisses the bankruptcy or issues an order lifting the stay and allowing you to proceed.

Some bankruptcy petitions result in liquidation, and the subject property will be sold to pay off creditors and liens. When this happens, you will be paid off as a secured creditor because your lien is secured by the property.

Other bankruptcy petitions result in reorganization of debts, and the bankruptcy court approves a payment plan that may provide for monthly payments to pay off a tax lien over a six-year period. During this period of time, the court sets reasonable interest that generally should be equal to the amount you would otherwise accrue on your tax lien.

There are many other issues that arise when a property owner files for bankruptcy, but they are beyond the purposes of this book.

Property with No Value

Thankfully, this is a rare problem. Property values generally have been rising, and almost all property is highly valued. Notice that I used the word *almost*. Some property has little or no resale value.

Property that has been designated as wetlands cannot be used for anything. You can't build or even farm on wetlands, so it is essentially worthless. Some lots are obviously swamp and their value is apparent, but other times appearances may be deceiving. The only way to be sure about whether a property is designated as wetlands is to check with the local building department's wetlands delineation map. Sometimes, even the map doesn't help because the maps do not include the block and lot designations. It can be very difficult to determine where a particular parcel is located on the wetlands map. Ask the staff of the building department for help, but if there is any doubt, don't buy the lien.

Properties that have been polluted and are environmentally contaminated are often without any value. The cost of cleaning up the property can easily exceed the ultimate resale value. Federal and state laws require the owner or polluter to clean up these properties, but that always takes many years, and the responsible party often cannot be found or simply cannot afford to clean up the property.

Other lots can be worthless based on their size or physical condition. Some lots simply cannot be profitably used or developed because they are on the side of a steep embankment, or they are too small to develop under applicable zoning restrictions.

The easiest way to avoid the risk of valueless property is to only buy liens on developed property. Once a property is improved with a structure, that building is permitted to remain in use regardless of changes in wetlands delineation or zoning requirements.

Diminishing Property Value

Always keep in mind that you will only get that attractive high interest rate *IF* the lien is redeemed. If it is not redeemed, you get the property. Usually that is good news— very good news. But it can be bad news if the property has a market value less than the redemption value of your lien. The vast majority of tax liens never grow big enough to approach the property value, but there are exceptions. I have foreclosed on many liens where the investor lost money on the sale of the property.

Accordingly, determining and monitoring the value of the property is an import-ant part of this investment vehicle. If a building is damaged or destroyed after you buy a lien on it, you may have a problem. Houses are sometimes left abandoned and open to the weather during foreclosure proceedings. This usually results in frozen pipes, water damage, vandalism, and theft by trespassers. One of my clients found a bear living in an abandoned house that we were foreclosing on. Bears don't pay rent, and they are hard to evict!

A tax certificate represents only a lien; no immediate possessory rights are trans-ferred until foreclosure is completed. Thus, a tax lien holder is generally not entitled to enter upon the underlying property to analyze, manage, or protect it.

Regardless of what happens, tax lien investors generally have a safety net in that the ground itself has value that is hard to destroy. The house may blow away in a storm or be knocked down during a rowdy frat party, but the ground will remain. As long as it isn't environmentally impaired with contamination or wetlands, the ground itself usually has value that exceeds the tax lien.

Once you foreclose and become the owner of a property, you will be responsible to address any Municipal Code Violations. It should not be surprising that property owners who lose their property to tax foreclosure are not known for maintaining their property. As the new owner, you will almost immediately begin receiving notices to clean up the yard, mow the overgrown grass, repair the fence, or board up the win-dows. As soon as the borough officials learn that there is a responsible new owner, they tend to jump right on you. This seems unfair, but they are just doing their job, trying to get a distressed property back in shape.

Along the same lines, if a municipality determines that a building presents a hazard to the community, it may issue a demolition order for the structure to be torn down. As the holder of a recorded lien, you are entitled to receive notice and appear at a hear-ing to determine whether the building must be demolished.

If a demolition order is issued and the building is torn down, the borough will impose a new first-priority lien on the property to recover the cost of the demolition. The result is that you will still hold your lien on the property, but now the structure will be gone and there will be another lien with higher priority ahead of you. As with any subsequent lien, you will either have to pay it off and add it to your lien, or it will be sold at the next tax auction. The new lien will continue to accrue interest and grow until it forecloses you out or you pay it off.

Widows and Orphans

The widows and orphans issue must be included in any consideration of what can go wrong. Anyone investing in tax liens must come to terms with the fact that, if they stay at it long enough, they will find themselves in a position of foreclosing and evicting a widow, or a single mom, or someone with a serious illness, or some other heart-wrenching soul.

Hungry for More?

The more you learn, the better equipped you'll be to avoid pitfalls and to take advantage of opportunities. As I explained at the beginning of this chapter, this is by no means intended to provide a complete overview of tax lien investing. It would be impossible to include everything in a single chapter. The most successful tax lien investors have spent years gaining experience and studying this unique field. Never make the mistake of thinking that you know everything. There is always more to learn, so go look for it.

If you are the type who likes to get information directly from the source, you can read the tax lien statutes in your state, but there are many books on this subject, including:

Tax Sale Certificates: A Review of the Tax Sale Law (Volume 26, *Seton Hall Law Review* 1607);

- ✓ *Tax Liens$, The Complete Guide to Investing in New Jersey Tax Liens*, Pellegrino, 2005;
- ✓ *The 16% Solution*, Moskowitz, 1994;
- ✓ *Tax Lien Investing Secrets*, Musa 2015;
- ✓ *Profit by Investing in Real Estate Tax Liens*, Loftis 2005

2

Peer-to-Peer Lending
Making Small Unsecured Loans

What do you think of this investment opportunity? You loan your hard-earned cash to a stranger whom you will never meet. The loan is unsecured, so you will not hold a mortgage lien or any type of collateral to secure the repayment of the loan. If the borrower defaults, you cannot file a collection lawsuit. You will have no control over the collection efforts. A third-party servicer (who arranged the loan) will decide whether to make any collection efforts, or write off the loan on your behalf. Sound appealing? Of course not, but don't turn to the next chapter just yet: you may feel differently if you read the next few pages. After accounting for defaults, investors who diversify among many small loans can make *net returns of 5 to 10 percent just sitting at a computer*.

Summary Points

1. **Specialized Knowledge:** None
2. **Minimum Capital Requirement:** $2,500
3. **Scalability:** Yes
4. **Liquidity:** Limited; resale of the accounts is not well organized
5. **Priority over other forms of debt:** Not secured by a lien
6. **Barriers to Entry:** Not available in some states, and in some States open only to "Qualified Investors"

What is Peer-to-Peer Lending?

Peer-to-peer lenders such as Lending Club and Prosper provide online marketplaces that originate loans of up to $35,000 and offer investors an opportunity to participate by financing a portion of the loan. Their goal is to "disrupt" or transform the traditional bank lending industry to reduce costs and increase transparency and efficiency. Through their websites, they connect borrowers and investors and provide related services including screening and grading borrowers, and collecting and processing monthly payments for the investors.

The idea is simple and appealing: ***Use the Internet to cut out the middleman (banks) from typical loans***. Under the traditional banking system, investors deposit their extra money in banks and earn a very low interest rate (recently under 1 percent). The bank then loans the funds to borrowers at higher rates of interest based on the borrower's credit history. The bank sets the interest rate based on various factors such as the borrower's credit score, income level, employment history, and the length of the loan. Higher risk loans earn higher interest to offset the higher risk of default. The bank takes on the risk of default, collects the loan payments, and makes a profit based on the difference between the low interest rate that it pays to investors for their deposits and the high interest rate that it charges on the loans.

The peer-to-peer investment model allows the investor to take on the role of the banker and earn an attractive rate of interest. In some ways, it is the Uber of loans.

What about the Risk of Default?

For hundreds of years, banks have used a variety of lending criteria to evaluate credit risk, and these techniques are not secret. P2P lenders such as Lending Club and Prosper evaluate each proposed loan and rank them based on the same criteria that the banks apply. The loans are screened, graded, and assigned an interest rate that reflects the level of risk. Of course, the riskiest loans are weeded out and rejected.

Investors then review the graded loans and select loans in which to participate. Members have access to the borrower's credit data including income level, FICO score, default history, and debt load. One of the best features is that you do not have to provide funding for the entire loan. Most investors elect to "participate" in many loans by funding small pieces of a lot of loans. Investors may invest ***as little as $25*** in a loan to spread the risk among many loans.

If a loan is fully funded by investors, then the servicer closes the loan and manages the monthly payments. Monthly payments of principal and interest are transferred into the investor's account. If there aren't enough investors willing to pitch in to fund a loan, then the loan is rejected.

Why Investors Should Consider This

Peer-to-peer lending has gained popularity and seems to be here to stay. This is a relatively new and unknown investment, but it is growing rapidly. The two leading "P2P" platforms, Prosper and Lending Club, were formed in 2006 and 2007, respectively. They started slowly, finding their way through the recession, but as of September 30, 2016 Lending Club has originated over $22 billion in loans, and Prosper has loaned over $6 billion. The chart below reveals the rapid pace of growth in P2P loans:

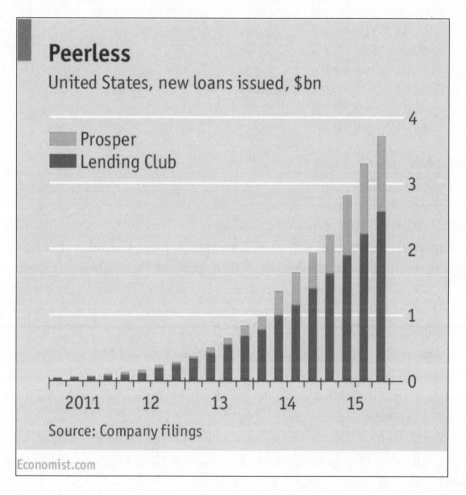

Peerless
United States, new loans issued, $bn

■ Prosper
■ Lending Club

2011   12   13   14   15

Source: Company filings

Economist.com

Returns have been attractive. According to figures posted by Prosper (chart below) on its website, its highest graded loans have generated a net return of $5.48 percent. The "AA" graded loans carried a 7.09 percent yield and had a 1.61 percent rate of write-offs, which left a net yield of 5.48 percent. Lower graded loans generated higher profits even though they suffered higher loss rates, because the interest rates on the higher risk loans offset the higher loss rate.

Seasoned Returns as of September 30, 2014

For Loans Originated July 2009 - November 2013

Prosper Rating	# Loans	$ Amount Loans	Average Loan Amount	Actual Effective Yield	Actual Loss Rate	Actual Return	Weighted Avg FICO Score
AA	3,995	$43,669,147	$10,931	7.09%	1.61%	**5.48%**	769
A	10,611	$115,364,446	$10,872	9.97%	3.19%	**6.78%**	726
B	11,544	$125,189,659	$10,845	14.02%	4.54%	**9.47%**	708
C	13,325	$130,555,564	$9,798	17.68%	6.55%	**11.14%**	691
D	12,553	$86,445,079	$6,886	21.69%	10.95%	**10.74%**	679
E	8,511	$37,251,026	$4,377	25.31%	13.97%	**11.35%**	668
HR	6,751	$23,327,191	$3,455	26.81%	16.04%	**10.78%**	664
Total:	67,290	$561,802,112	$8,349	15.94%	6.62%	**9.33%**	703

Prosper.com

Some deep-pocketed investors have taken notice. In 2013, Google led a round of private investors that bought a $125 million stake in Lending Club, valuing the company at over $1.5 billion. Lending Club then went public in late 2014. Prosper also landed a $20 million investment from Sequoia Capital. Goldman Sachs has launched its own direct lending site, called Marcus. There are many P2P sites in Europe, China, Japan, and India, as well.

Unfortunately, P2P lending is a relatively new asset class and has not been approved for investors in every state. More states are being added, so check the P2P websites for an updated status on your home state. As of the writing of this book, the following states allow residents to participate:

Alaska, Arizona, California, Colorado, Connecticut, Delaware, Florida, Georgia, Hawaii, Idaho, Illinois, Indiana, Iowa, Kansas, Kentucky, Louisiana, Maine, Massachusetts, Minnesota, Mississippi, Montana, Nebraska, Nevada, New Hampshire, New Jersey, New York, Oklahoma, Rhode Island, South Dakota, Texas, Utah, Vermont, Virginia, Washington, West Virginia, Wisconsin, Wyoming.

Why Aren't Default Rates Higher?

Unsecured loans are very hard to enforce and collect, so investors often wonder why there isn't a higher rate of default. Why are these borrowers paying off their loans? The answer seems to be that the credit system simply works. Banks have proven that this model works through their credit cards—which are unsecured, low-balance consumer debt, just like P2P loans. There are two strong factors at work to keep defaults down. First, the peer-to-peer sites screen the borrowers (just like the credit card companies) and weed out the borrowers who are most likely to default. Borrowers with the worst credit history do not make it onto the P2P sites. Second, borrowers have strong incentive to pay back the loans in order to preserve their credit scores. Our society has become more and more reliant on credit. Borrowers are well aware of the negative impact that a default will have on their credit score—which will impact their lives for many years.

It is important to understand that all investors will suffer a percentage of defaults. Defaults are part of this investment, but as illustrated in the charts above, the default rate can be overcome by the high interest rates if the loan portfolio is properly diversified and spread out among many quality loans.

Why Borrowers Like P2P Lenders

Following the Great Recession of 2007–2009, it has become much harder for borrowers with imperfect credit ratings to obtain loans. Borrowers seem to be flocking to peer-to-peer lending as a simpler, lower-cost, and faster option. The borrower fills out forms online explaining the purpose of the loan, authorizing a credit history check, and selecting the term of the loan—either 36 or 60 months. Then, if the loan passes the servicer's initial screening, the loan will be listed on the website for investors to review and select. If the loan is fully funded by investors, then the borrower signs loan documents and the loan proceeds are transferred into the borrower's account. Monthly payments of principal and interest are automatically transferred from the borrower's bank account, and the borrower may pay off the loan early without penalty.

The entire process is done online so borrowers avoid embarrassing, time-consuming meetings with bank loan officers. The online application takes twenty to thirty minutes to complete. Minutes later, the borrower receives preapproval (or rejection), and the proposed loan (of up to $35,000) is assigned a grade and an interest rate. If the borrower accepts the terms, then the loan is posted for investors to select. If investors choose to fund it, the loan can be approved and funded into the borrower's bank account within days. Traditional banks cannot match that convenience, transparency, and efficiency.

The borrower's identity is never disclosed to the investors, so there is no opportunity for investors to contact the borrower if the loan is defaulted. Collection efforts, if any, are managed by the P2P lender. The typical collection process includes in-house phone calls and/or letters, then referral to a collection agency, and then possibly referral to a collection law firm. These loans are unsecured, so collection efforts may not be cost-efficient. The P2P lender retains full discretion as to what collection efforts (if any) are warranted.

Borrowers apply for these peer-to-peer loans for a wide variety of purposes including consolidation of credit card debt, to start or expand a small business, to make home repairs, for higher education, or even for vacation expenses. Lending Club has fourteen predefined purposes for borrowers to select:

1. Car
2. Credit Card
3. Debt Consolidation
4. Educational
5. Home Improvement
6. House
7. Major Purchase
8. Medical
9. Moving
10. Renewable Energy
11. Small Business
12. Vacation
13. Wedding
14. Other

The majority of borrowers indentify "debt consolidation" or "credit card" as the purpose, but the purpose is not validated or confirmed in any way. Investors must assume that many borrowers do not use the loan proceeds for the stated purpose.

The loan application process is very similar to a standard bank loan application, and if the loan is funded, the borrower can get an interest rate that is lower than a bank would charge. Lending Club reports that as of June 2015, the majority of borrowers use the loans to pay off high interest rate loans such as credit cards, and the average Lending Club borrower had the following loan data:

- 699 FICO score
- 17.7 percent debt-to-income ratio (excluding mortgage)
- 16.2 years of credit history
- $73,945 personal income (top 10 percent of US population)
- Average Loan Size: $14,553

The P2P servicer naturally charges the borrower an origination fee of 1 percent to 5 percent, depending on the grade of the loan. The servicer also charges a 1 percent processing fee for each monthly payment, and Prosper charges investors a 1 percent annual fee on all loan assets. This is how peer-to-peer sites make their money.

If This Is So Good, Why Isn't Everyone Doing It?

Fair question. There are a few reasons why most people have not heard of peer-to-peer lending. The main reason is that it is a relatively new investment class, introduced in 2006. It takes years for new investments to gain widespread acceptance, especially when brokers are not involved. Brokers generally educate their clients on investment products that generate a commission for the broker. P2P lending does not involve brokers, so there is no one out there pushing the opportunity. As illustrated in the charts above, however, this investment is taking off and is gaining more and more public acceptance.

Another reason that this investment has not gained widespread support is illustrated by the first paragraph of this chapter. This type of investment is not immediately appealing on the surface. Who would want to make unsecured consumer loans to strangers? It is only after an investor drills down into the details that P2P loans truly reveal their beauty. Most people simply do not do the work to discover the appeal of this opportunity.

How Do I Do This?

Getting started is easy. Just visit the website of one or all of the peer-to-peer lenders and open an account online. It takes just 5–10 minutes. You'll be asked to link a bank account in order to transfer funds back and forth, but you can opt to simply send a check.

Qualified Investors Only?

Unfortunately, some states do not allow peer-to-peer lending. You can invest if you are you a resident of: California, Colorado, Connecticut, Delaware, Florida, Georgia, Hawaii, Idaho, Illinois, Kentucky, Louisiana, Maine, Minnesota, Mississippi, Missouri, Montana, Nevada, New Hampshire, New Jersey, New York, North Dakota, Rhode Island, South Dakota, Texas, Utah, Vermont, Virginia, Washington, West Virginia, Wisconsin, and Wyoming. This issue seems to be in flux, so check with the P2P websites to confirm the latest rules on who may invest.

Depending where you live, there may be some net worth and income requirements. For example, in most states, investors must have either (1) gross annual income of $70,000 and have a net worth of $70,000, or (2) a net worth of $250,000 regardless of income. In some states, there are no restrictions.

Grading the Loans

Once you are a member, you can start to peruse the loans available for investment. The first step is to determine your personal risk tolerance. There is no correct answer here. Each grade of loan carries a different interest rate based on the risk level. Lending Club grades the loans from A (highest credit score) to G (lowest credit score):

Loan Grade	Interest Rate	Origination Fee	36-Month APR	60-Month APR
A	5.32% - 7.99%	1% - 5%*	5.99% - 11.51%	7.46% - 10.19%
B	8.24% - 11.49%	5%	11.77% - 15.08%	10.44% - 13.76%
C	12.74% - 15.99%	6%	17.12% - 20.46%	15.52% - 18.86%
D	16.99% - 21.49%	6%	21.48% - 26.11%	19.89% - 24.53%
E	19.99% - 26.24%	6%	24.57% - 31.00%	22.98% - 29.43%
F	24.24% - 30.74%	6%	28.94% - 35.63%	27.36% - 34.08%
G	28.55% - 30.99%	6%	33.37% - 35.89%	31.82% - 34.34%

Source: LendingClub.com

Investors have access to all of the borrower's credit information (other than the borrower's identity) and simply shop through the loans à la carte. Conservative investors can select higher-quality loans that carry less risk and lower interest in the mid-single digits, while more aggressive investors may be drawn to the higher risk loans that accrue interest at over 25 percent. These more aggressive investors understand that a larger portion of the loans will default, but they expect the high interest rate to more than make up for the default rate. Note that the chart above reflects the interest rates charged for each grade of loan. This is *not* the actual return that investors have earned after defaults are included.

Factoring In the Expected Default Rate

Of course, all P2P investors will suffer a percentage of defaults. It is unavoidable and will reduce profits. This risk cannot be entirely avoided but can be managed through loan selection. The chart below summarizes all Lending Club loans from 2007 to 2016. Each row reveals how the different grades of loans have performed after losses are charged off. You may be surprised to see that the lower-grade, higher-risk loans have generated higher net returns after factoring in defaults.

LOAN PERFORMANCE DETAILS

	TOTAL ISSUED	FULLY PAID	CURRENT	LATE	CHARGED OFF (NET)	PRINCIPAL PAYMENTS RECEIVED	INTEREST PAYMENTS RECEIVED	AVG. INTEREST RATE	ADJ. NET ANNUALIZED RETURN[1]
A:	$2,922,464,950	$852,626,814	$1,311,656,416	$10,723,228	$31,975,848	$1,568,158,222	$195,824,739	7.14%	5.18%
B:	$4,864,283,075	$1,422,089,792	$2,254,004,993	$40,234,578	$122,685,290	$2,447,358,206	$502,407,221	10.60%	6.91%
C:	$4,997,008,225	$1,236,483,718	$2,462,205,247	$80,130,206	$221,453,838	$2,233,218,926	$688,887,635	13.93%	7.62%
D:	$2,851,405,775	$721,541,245	$1,317,506,967	$69,435,197	$210,350,772	$1,254,112,833	$508,159,491	17.43%	7.46%
E:	$1,639,301,175	$386,316,598	$751,060,145	$59,542,540	$167,276,665	$661,421,823	$349,241,950	20.40%	6.82%
F: G	$743,200,600	$182,870,811	$309,047,748	$34,456,547	$107,708,374	$291,987,893	$185,295,626	24.53%	5.34%
ALL:	$18,017,663,800	$4,801,928,978	$8,405,481,516	$294,522,296	$861,450,787	$8,456,257,903	$2,429,816,661	13.51%	6.85%

Prosper similarly grades on a scale of AA to E (with an extra category of HR for high risk). On its webpage, Prosper provides the historic loss rate for each grade of loan based on the past performance of Prosper loans with similar characteristics. The highest-rated "AA" loans have a historic loss rate of under 2 percent, while the highest-risk loans have a loss rate of over 15 percent.

Prosper Rating	Estimated Avg. Annual Loss Rate
AA	0.00-1.99%
A	2.00–3.99%
B	4.00–5.99%
C	6.00–8.99%
D	9.00–11.99%
E	12.00–14.99%
HR	≥ 15.00%

The estimated loss rates are not a guarantee and actual performance may differ from expected performance, but this sheds light on the risk associated with each grade level. Of course, the lower-grade loans accrue higher interest to make up for the higher default rate.

Some Flaws with Historic Stats

Some statistics and charts on default rates may be less significant than they seem, due to the enormous increase in the number of peer-to-peer loans in recent years. Most loans don't default immediately—it takes time to see if a given loan will default. Because a large percentage of all P2P loans are relatively fresh (issued in the past six to twelve months), these fresh loans have not ripened to the point of default yet, so they skew the statistics. In other words, a fresh loan that just closed last month should not be included in default stats because it has not aged long enough to carry any weight in a statistical analysis.

Most stats on default rates typically do not take this "aging" into account. The most accurate statistics only evaluate aged loans—leaving out loans that were originated in the past two years. The ideal stats are based only on loans for which the term has been completed. Both Prosper and Lending Club provide loads of data and charts on their sites, and it is critical for investors to spend some time to gain an understanding of past performance. There are also a few independent websites (listed at the end of this chapter) that provide great analysis. As you review historic statistics, note that Lending Club changed its credit model in 2008, so older data may not be applicable. The best data are based on loans that were originated after 2008 with terms that have been completed.

A lot has been written about default rates and loan purposes. There seems to be a pattern of higher default rates for loans with a stated purpose of business, education, renewable energy, moving expenses, and medical expenses. These statistics are of questionable value for two reasons. First, the loan purpose is not verified. Second, the majority of loans are clustered in the area of debt consolidation and credit cards, so the other purposes may be statistically insignificant.

Perhaps the biggest issue with P2P default statistics is the short history of this sector. P2P lending is no new that we don't have decades of default statistics to evaluate.

Diversifying Your Portfolio of Loans

Diversity is an advantage for any type of investment because in simplest terms, it spreads the risk. There are a few ways to diversify a loan portfolio. In order to spread the risk of default, investors can spread their funds among many loans. The minimum participation is just $25 per loan, and most investors take advantage of this feature to spread their investment among dozens of loans.

Investors also can also increase diversity by selecting loans among different grade levels—sprinkling in a few lower-grade loans to increase the return, while not wading too deeply into the higher-risk loans. The loan term is another variable that can be mixed in. Longer-term loans generally accrue higher interest. The loans are all relatively short term—twelve, thirty-six, or sixty months—and monthly payments are deposited directly into the investor's account to be either reinvested into more loans or transferred to the investor's bank account.

Diversification can also be increased by investing through a variety of P2P platforms. You don't have to stick with Lending Club just because it is the largest. Look into spreading your money around among other sites that offer other types of loans, such as small business loans and accounts receivable loans.

Selecting Your Loans

There are a few ways to build a portfolio of loans. Investors can select individual loans or use an automated feature that selects loans for you based on criteria that you set. Sifting through the list of available loans is interesting and educational at first, but if you plan to invest a lot and spread your money among many loans, the process can get tedious rather quickly. It is important for beginners to spend time getting familiar with the data available on borrowers, so every new investor should start out analyzing loans one at a time.

After you get the hang of the process by acquiring several loans, you'll start to develop your own criteria for choosing loans that appeal to you. Aside from the grading system described above, there are plenty of data available to sift through. You can set the filters to help narrow down your targets.

Here are the common filters. These filters can be a bit overwhelming, so before you wade into these, keep in mind that these credit factors have already been incorporated into the grade and interest rate set by Lending Club or Prosper. Some investors don't use the filters at all because they feel that the grading system already reflects the details that the filters address. In any event, here is a list of the common filters offered by Lending Club:

✓ **Interest Rate:** As discussed in detail above, lower grades accrue higher interest rates. Both Lending Club and Prosper post historic returns for each grade level so investors can easily determine expected default rates and net returns for each grade level. I don't think there is a right or wrong decision on this issue. It comes down to a personal tolerance for risk. If defaults are going to keep you up at night and drive you away from this investment option, then select higher-grade, lower-interest loans. On the other hand, if you can stomach the higher rate of defaults that comes along with the higher interest rates, then swing for the fences. I suggest a diversified portfolio that mixes some lower-grade loans into a pool of mostly high-grade loans.

✓ **Loan Purpose:** The most commonly stated purpose for the loan is debt consolidation (typically paying off higher-interest credit cards). Many investors like this and take it as a sign of financial responsibility and good intentions. Many investors shy away from loans to start or expand a small business because of the risk of failure.

✓ **Max Loan Amount:** Smaller loans are easier to pay off, but if other factors are all strong, then a larger loan may be acceptable.

✓ **Review Status:** All loans are reviewed by the P2P servicer before the loan is closed, but some loans are fully reviewed before the investors fully fund the loan. This is preferable to avoid wasting time on loans that will not ultimately be approved. However, the other side of this argument is that some very attractive loans just aren't fully reviewed and approved until after the loan is fully funded. If you wait for the approval process, you may miss out on the chance to invest in that loan.

✓ **Verified Income:** Unfortunately, the borrower's income is not always verified. It is obviously a plus when the income is verified.

✓ **Funding Progress:** This shows the level of interest from other investors. Once a loan is fully funded by other investors, it is too late for any other investors to participate.

✓ **Listing Expires in . . . :** Deadline for investors to decide whether to participate in this loan.

✓ **Exclude Relisted Loans:** If a loan is not fully funded, the borrower can apply to relist it, but investors may be wary about the reasons for which it was not funded the first time around. Attractive loans are typically fully funded in the first offering.

✓ **Credit Score:** One of the most critical factors. Higher is better, but look for at least 680.

✓ **Max Debt-to-Income Ratio:** I find this filter to be a bit misleading because it does not include all debt; for example, mortgage payments are not included in this calculation. Ten percent to 15 percent is preferred.

- ✓ **Earliest Credit Line:** I'd prefer at least a ten-year credit history. Lenders cannot discriminate by age, but this information provides a clue as to whether the borrower is a kid that has not been established yet.
- ✓ **Open Credit Lines:** Less is better. Under 10 is standard.
- ✓ **Total Credit Lines:** Less is better.
- ✓ **Revolving Credit Balance:** Less is better. Under $50,000 is preferred.
- ✓ **Revolving Balance Utilization**: Less is better. Under 50 percent is preferred. Avoid borrowers who have already maxed out their available credit.
- ✓ **Inquiries in the last six months:** Less is better. One or zero is preferable.
- ✓ **Months since Last Delinquency:** Less is better. Zero is preferable.
- ✓ **Months since Last Record:** Public records include big negative events like bankruptcy or defaulting on a loan. Any record in the last few years is a bad sign.
- ✓ **Home Ownership:** Considered a sign of responsibility and a positive factor.
- ✓ **Length of Employment:** Three to five years is preferred, but no less than one year.
- ✓ **Location State**: Not critical, but some investors seek to diversify by region or target regions with stronger-growing local economies. I recommend diversifying by region because local economies are subject to swift reversals caused by natural disasters.
- ✓ **Keyword:** Investors can screen loans by any term that they are looking for.
- ✓ **Public Records:** This filter seems to overlap with the "Months since Last Record" filter above, but it allows investors to screen out borrowers with any public record such as bankruptcy of default regardless of the date. Any public record is a bad sign.
- ✓ **Delinquencies (Last two years):** The number of reported delinquencies in recent years is important. There is an old proverb warning against trying to "catch a falling knife." I like to see no reported delinquencies in the past two years, but if everything else is strong, an exception may be warranted.
- ✓ **Exclude Loans already Invested In:** This filter eliminates loans that you have already reviewed and funded. It helps diversify a portfolio by preventing investors from accidentally contributing more funds into a loan that they have already agreed to fund.
- ✓ **Loan Term:** Shorter term 12- or 36-month loans have less risk but also accrue interest about 2 percent lower than similar loans that are for 60 months. A conservative approach would be to stay short term.
- ✓ **Initial Listing Status:** Most investors set this screen for "fractional." It allows investors to search for loans that are offered as a whole or in fractions. Most P2P investors seek small fractions of loans rather than funding an entire loan.

- ✓ **Monthly Income:** Filters by the borrower's monthly income. Verified income is a plus.
- ✓ **Loan ID**: Allows investors to search for a specific loan by its ID listing. This is useful if you are referring a friend to a particular loan.
- ✓ **Recent Listings**: This screens for the most recently listed new loans.
- ✓ **Collections excluding Medical:** Any entries for collections on a borrower's record would be a red flag.
- ✓ **Major Derogatory:** This weeds out borrowers who have had a major negative mark on their credit report.

Again, keep in mind that these factors have already been considered when the "grade" was assigned to each loan, so don't get too bogged down if some of these seem to be overly technical.

The flow of new loans is not steady, so be patient and keep checking back for new loans that fit your own personal criteria. If you find that your filters do not produce any loans over a period of time, then your filters are not set in a realistic model. You will not find high-interest loans with impeccable credit history. Try to reset the filters, or perhaps this investment is not fitting for you. There are plenty of other places in which to invest your funds.

Secondary Market

Lending Club has established a secondary market called FOLIOfn for investors to sell loans to one another. The process is not as smooth as it is for buying a fresh loan, and buyers are appropriately skeptical about buying a loan that is being "unloaded" or "dumped" by another investor. Despite this hurdle, it is worth checking out.

Consider selling a loan if the borrower is late in making one or more monthly payments. There is a "grace period" for late payments before the loan is considered to be in default, but a pattern of late "grace period" payments often leads to a default. It is better to try to unload the loan before it goes into default.

Secured P2P Investing

Some peer-to-peer lenders even offer loans that are secured by a lien on real property or the debtor's assets. These sites, like Realtyshares.com, Sharestates.com, Realtymogul.com, Patchofland.com, and many others link up investors with borrowers for mortgage loans to participate in mortgage loans. Uhaulinvestorsclub.com allows investors to participate in loans to the parent company of U-Haul, and the loans are secured by U-Haul's trucks, trailers, or equipment. There are a lot of options, and more keep springing up.

Default Insurance?

The largest peer-to-peer firms, Lending Club and Prosper, currently do not offer any insurance or "provision funds" to cover the risk of defaults, but perhaps that option will be available in the near future. Zopa and RateSetter are two P2P lending outfits in the UK, and they came up with a clever option for protection against defaults. A percentage of fees for all loans go into a trust fund to cover default losses (when borrowers fail to repay their loan). Of course, there is no guarantee that the "default provisions" would be enough to cover all losses if default rates were to increase, but as I write this chapter, both lenders state that their programs have covered all defaulted loans. Again, nothing is free, so keep in mind that the cost of this "loss coverage" comes at the cost of lower returns. In essence, it just spreads the risk of default and covers it through fees. Unfortunately, Zopa and RateSetter are only available to investors who live in the United Kingdom. I like the idea and expect Lending Club and Prosper to eventually offer a similar option.

Tips from a Pro

I asked my friend George Alex Popescu to provide some expert insight on P2P lending. George is the founder, CEO, and editor in chief of *Lending Times*, a media company that publishes in the peer-to-peer and alternative lending space (LendingTimes.com)

George Alex Popescu:

The best advice that I could give any investor is to put some real thought into diversifying to manage risk. Investing in peer-to-peer loans is already a great way gain diversity from your other investment such as real estate, stocks, and bonds. Most new P2P investors spread their funds among many small loans, and that is a great start. Investors

---

should strive for even better diversity by spreading funds among a few different platforms. I invest through Lending Club and Prosper, but I like to spread my risk by also investing through other P2P companies. In fact, I prefer P2P loans that are secured by real property. I have written a lot on this subject in the *Lending Times,* which can be accessed online for free.

Lack of liquidity can also be an issue for some new investors. If you buy into a three-year note, you'd better be absolutely sure that you won't need your money back sooner. I have heard of many investors who suffered big losses trading out of their notes early. Think of these notes like a bank CD that you cannot cash in until the term is up.

Finally, consider investing through your IRA to save on taxes.

Over the last ten years, George founded ten companies in online lending, craft beer brewery, exotic sports car rental space, hedge funds, peer-reviewed scientific journal, etc. He has advised dozens of early stage start-ups in different fields and was a mentor at MIT's Venture Mentoring Services and Techstars Fintech in New York. In short, he knows his stuff.

What Can Go Wrong? Common Pitfalls to Avoid

The most common error that investors seem to make is reaching too far for higher interest rates. As with most investments, higher reward carries higher risk. When reviewing the list of loans, your eye will naturally be drawn to the rates in the high teens, and investors can be guided by greed into a portfolio loaded with defaults. An experienced and disciplined investor will study the historic rates of default and net return for each grade level and then select a portfolio of loans that fits his or her risk tolerance. Keep in mind that *historic* rates of default may not continue. As the economy cycles up and down, default rates will change.

Another common pitfall is failure to diversify among many loans. Simply put, don't put too many eggs in one basket. Both of the major P2P platforms allow investments of as little as $25 per loan, so take advantage of that and spread your funds out as much as possible. Never fall in love with any single loan regardless of how much it may appear to be a "sure thing." Also, consider spreading your funds among a few different P2P lenders.

Summary of the Pros & Cons

Pros

✓ **High Interest:** Interest income is comparably high in comparison to similar investments.

✓ **Diversity:** Investment in consumer loans provides a hedge against other investment asset classes such stock or bonds.

✓ **Control:** Investors manage risk and income through individual selection of loans-based filters and loan grading.

✓ **Spreading Risk:** Investors may diversify with many loans at low ($25) values to spread the risk of default.

✓ **Automated Option:** Investors may use automated models to build portfolios of loans-based on preset models

✓ **Time, Funds, & Expertise:** Unlike many of the investment options discussed in this book, peer-to-peer lending does not require a lot of time, money, or experience. Investors can start with just $100, and the websites make the process quick and easy.

✓ **Helping Others:** Loans that investors fund may help the borrower pay for education or pay off higher interest loans.

✓ **Scalability:** It is exceptionally easy to scale up this investment from $100 to $100,000. Management of many loans is especially easy though the automated investment option.

✓ **Cash Flow:** Interest payments are transferred directly into investor's account each month.

✓ **Taxes:** Although the interest income is fully taxable at the investor's income tax rate, investors may open accounts through an IRA or Roth IRA to shelter the income.

✓ **Stability:** No "market swings" like the stock market or mutual funds.

✓ **Professional Assistance:** The P2P sites prescreen and grade loans for investors, process and distribute the monthly payments, and manage the collection process upon default.

Cons

✓ **Interest rate fluctuations:** As interest rates increase in the generate market, the value of fixed-interest loans decreases. This risk applies to all fixed-rate income investments.

✓ **Risk of Default:** Unlike a bank deposit or bank CD, these loans are not FDIC-insured. There is no guarantee of repayment. Borrowers will default on a percentage of loans, and it will reduce the investor's return. Additionally, the grading supplied by Lending Club and Prosper may be inaccurate, underestimating default risks.

✓ **Control:** Investors have no control over collection efforts when loans default.

✓ **Unpredictable Cash Flow:** All loans may be paid off by the borrower at any time, so future cash flow and interest may be unpredictable.

✓ **Untested:** Relatively new asset class has not been tested through long-term economic cycles. Periodic recessions will have negative impact on default rates.

✓ **Illiquid:** This is a long-term investment. The loans are for three- or five-year terms. Although there is a secondary market to resell loans, it could take weeks to cash out, and the resale value is based subject to demand from other investors.

✓ **Fees:** Lending Club and Prosper charge fees for collection efforts and payment processing. The fees could be increased in the future.

✓ **Restrictions:** Not available to investors in some states, and in some states investors must be financially qualified.

✓ **Security & Priority:** These loans are unsecured and low priority in collection efforts. They may be eliminated through bankruptcy and are behind all other secured debt such as mortgages and tax liens.

✓ **Failure of the Servicer.** While it seems unlikely, it is possible that Lending Club, Prosper, or any of the other peer-to-peer lending companies could fail and file bankruptcy. The underlying loans should not be directly affected and there are contingencies in place for orderly liquidation, but this could disrupt cash flow to investors.

Publicly Traded Alternatives

On-Deck Capital : ONDK

Lending Club : LC

Hungry for More? Source Books, Consultants, Websites, and Sellers

Peer-to-Peer Lending Sites:

lendingclub.com

prosper.com

ondeck.com

Uhaulinvestorsclub.com

Realtyshares.com

Sharestates.com

Realtymogul.com

Patchofland.com

Books:

A Beginner's Guide to Lending Club, Adam Davidson

Building Wealth through Peer-to-Peer Lending, David Shipman

Cutting Out the Banks with Peer Lending, Dale Poyser

How to Profit from Peer-to-Peer Lending, Scott Todd

The Lending Club Story, Peter Renton

The Complete Idiot's Guide to Person-To-Person Lending, Beverly Harzog and
    Curtis Arnold

Understanding Peer-to-Peer-Lending, Peter Renton

Websites:

Lendingtimes.com

Lendacademy.com

Nickelsteamroller.com

Peercube.com

Lendingrobot.com

3

Credit Card Debt
Buying and Collecting Defaulted Credit Card Debt

redit cards are a useful tool for many, a financial disaster for some, and perhaps a great investment opportunity for you. Most people are shocked to hear that you can invest in credit card debt. It is truly a well-kept secret. Over the last ten years, I have invested over $2.2 million in defaulted credit card accounts totaling over $12 million in debt, and I've managed to collect $4.8 million from those accounts so far. That is over a 100 percent return on investment, and money is still flowing in. I have spent countless hours analyzing and refining this process, and I've tried to summarize it all here.

Summary Points

1. **Specialized Knowledge:** Property valuation, searching public records
2. **Minimum Capital Requirement:** $5,000 and up
3. **Scalability:** Yes
4. **Liquidity:** Limited; resale of the accounts is not well organized
5. **Priority over Other Forms of Debt:** Low; credit cards are not liens but are converted into low priority judgment liens on real property in many states
6. **Barriers to Entry:** Must be a "Qualified/ Accredited Investor"

This chapter will show you how to buy defaulted credit card debt at a deep discount, typically 5 percent to 20 percent of the debt. We will discuss how to find, screen, and buy the accounts, and how to convert the debt into an income stream secured by a lien on real property.

Credit card debt is a big problem that is not going away. As I write this chapter, the Federal Reserve estimates that total US credit card debt will reach a record high of $1 trillion by the end of 2016. The average family carries about $15,300 of credit card debt, and $132,000 in total debt. This high level of debt is a continuing trend. Equifax reported that 60 million new credit cards were issued in 2015, the highest level since the great recession.

Years ago, banks held their own defaulted credit card debt and tried to collect or restructure the debt "in house." Recent federal regulations, however, impose strong incentives for banks to sell off "bad debt," so banks sell their defaulted credit card debt, typically in huge multimillion-dollar pools. The large credit card companies typically "charge off" and sell between 3 to 4 percent of their credit card portfolio each year. But don't shed any tears for them; these losses are low compared to the high interest rates that the banks accrue on the remaining 96–97 percent of credit cards that are not written off and sold.

The finance companies that buy these portfolios usually "work" the accounts briefly and then "flip" them in smaller screened pools to smaller investors and collection companies known as "debt buyers."

Secured by Liens on Real Property?

Debt investors always think about "liens" and "priority," which are critical factors in collecting a debt.

A *lien* secures a debt by attaching the debt to the debtor's asset such as real estate.

Priority is the order in which liens are satisfied from the collateral. You can think of priority as the strength of the lien, A lien can be weak or strong, depending on its priority. This is critical because the collateral often is not valuable enough to satisfy all of the liens.

Credit card debt is ***unsecured***, so there is no lien on any asset to secure repayment. That makes it harder to collect or enforce this type of debt, and it justifies the low price that is typically paid for defaulted credit card debt. In most states, however, credit card debt can be converted into secured debt under certain circumstances:

1. A collection lawsuit results in a judgment for a sum of money;
2. The judgment is docketed as a lien; and
3. The debtor owns real property.

In most states, a money judgment from a collection suit becomes a lien on any real property that the debtor owns. Now as a ***secured*** debt, your odds of being paid are much higher. If the debtor wants to sell or refinance the property, your lien will be discovered, and you will have to be paid before the property can be sold or refinanced. Time is on your side as long as there is equity in the property.

Check with your local attorney to confirm this procedure in your state.

If This Is So Good . . .

Why isn't everyone buying this stuff? For more detail on this issue, turn back to the introductory discussion in this book, but in short, it boils down to barriers to entry. There are no commissions for investment advisors; only accredited investors can buy, and a little specialized knowledge is required.

There are also some net worth and income requirements. In most states, investors must have either a net worth of at least one million US dollars, excluding the value of one's primary residence, or have income at least $200,000 each year for the last two years (or $300,000 combined income if married).

How This Is Done

The first step is to contact a reseller and apply to be an approved buyer. Sellers have their own application forms, but they basically want to establish your identity and that you are qualified as an accredited investor.

There are many reputable resellers that buy credit card debt in huge batches and then resell it in smaller bundles after they have worked the accounts for a period of time. The Debt Buyers Association is the leading industry group in this field, and you can find a list of debt buyers and sellers on their website, DBAInternational.org. Not all of the listed debt buyers also sell accounts, so I suggest that you contact a few in your region. I have bought the majority of my accounts from Unifund CCR, LLC, based in Cincinnati, Ohio, and I found them to be straightforward and trustworthy, but I make no recommendations as to which seller is best for you. Personally, I worked with Unifund the most because of the flexibility that they offer in sorting and selecting accounts. For example, I only buy accounts where the debtor owns real property in certain counties within my state, and Unifund allows me to sort based on these criteria. I suggest that you check around and find a variety of sellers that meet your preferences.

After you have registered with one or more resellers, the next step is to request a portfolio to review. Sellers use different formats, but the lists are typically presented as a spreadsheet that includes:

- Amount due in principal and interest
- Applicable interest rate
- Date that the credit card account was opened
- Date of default
- Date that the account was "charged off" by the credit card company
- Account number
- Debtor's home municipality and county
- Name of the credit card company

The debtor's full name, address, and social security number are typically redacted (omitted) at this stage, but that sensitive information is provided after you have made a preliminary review and agree on a price and size of a purchase. Then the "unmasked" list is provided for your full review and diligence.

Portfolios of defaulted credit card debt can be bought at deep discounts of between 3–20 percent of the debt, depending on the criterion that you set. These portfolios are second- or third-hand, which means that two or three larger companies have owned or attempted to collect the accounts. None of the accounts, however, have been put into suit with attorneys.

Portfolios of accounts can be screened to increase the likelihood of collection, but this increases the cost of the accounts. Most marketers of this type of debt will only break it down by state and amount due. Some, like Unifund, will allow you to buy accounts based on the following factors:

Statute Date

This is the date by which the applicable statute of limitations expires. The statute of limitations is law that prohibits collection lawsuits after a certain date. Once an account reaches that "age," no lawsuit can be filed to collect the debt. Believe it or not, there is a market for buying and selling "out of date" debt. My model is to sue to collect the debt, so I never would buy debt that is beyond the statute of limitations.

Living Debtor

I always insist on accounts with living debtors, because it is much harder to collect from an estate.

Age of Debtor

It is easier to collect from a debtor in the prime earning ages of between 25 and 55.

Age of Debt

Fresh debt is more expensive to buy and easier to collect. My personal screening allows debt of any age—before the statute of limitations has expired.

1sts, 2nds, and 3rds

All credit card accounts have been previously owned and have been through collection efforts. A "1st" or "first" refers to "fresh" debt that is being sold for the first time. These first sales are in huge nationwide bundles sold to large multimillion-dollar buyers. I have never been offered or even seen "1-agency debt." By the time the accounts are broken down and sold to smaller local investors, they have been through at least one or more prior sales, so they are labeled 2nds or 3rds. A "three agency" or "3rd" account has been sold two or more times before.

Size of Accounts

It is always better to diversify your investments, so in my experience, it is better to buy many small accounts rather than a few large accounts. The old saying about putting too many eggs in one basket applies here. Accounts that are too small are not worth the time required to collect them. Large accounts carry too much risk—if they are uncollectable, it could kill the returns. I prefer accounts that are between $2,500 and $12,000.

Size of Portfolio

This relates to the overall size of the portfolio that you want to buy. Start with smaller batches to see how you do, but again, diversification is important, so don't go too small. I'd suggest at least $5,000 to $10,000.

Debtor's Location

Collection lawsuits generally must be filed in the county where the debtor resides. Debtors who live in counties that are economically thriving are more likely to be able to make payments. Increasing real estate values make it easier for the debtor to refinance and pay off debt.

Homeowner Accounts

I only buy accounts where the debtor owns real property. Unfortunately, most sellers will not allow buyers to screen based on property ownership. Unifund is the only reseller that I have found for "Homeowner Accounts." Of course, the price reflects this factor, so I pay more for Unifund's "homeowner" accounts than I'd have to pay for accounts from other sellers. I find it worth the extra cost because in my state (New Jersey), judgments are liens on all real property, so my debt becomes "secure" after I obtain a judgment. Check with your local collection attorney to confirm whether this applies in your location.

Once you and the seller agree on a set of factors of for screening accounts, and you agree on the overall size of your purchase, you will be provided with a list of accounts that has been partially redacted to hide details such as the debtors' names and social security numbers. You will then review the list and decide if you want to buy it. Most investors buy these accounts in the name of an LLC or corporation.

Debt Scoring

Many buyers get permission to run the proposed list of accounts through a "debt scoring." Scoring typically evaluates accounts based on the debtor's zip code and city demographics. It works best when comparing several large portfolios. The concept is simply that it is better to buy a portfolio of debt that includes more debtors in higher income areas, compared to a portfolio that includes more debtors in lower income areas. Of course it isn't perfect, but it can provide an edge in evaluating and comparing portfolios before you buy.

I generally have not run debt scores because I have always focused on "homeowner accounts," so my analysis is more focused on whether the debtor is really the property owner and whether there appears to be equity in the property. It is usually easier to collect from debtors who live in regions with stronger demographics, but I don't think it is worth the extra cost of credit scoring for debtors who own real estate. Many other investors do not agree with this approach, and they would never buy an account without having scored first. See what works best for you.

Be sure to negotiate for a long "return period" during which you can reject and return any accounts that you find are not in compliance with the screening factors that you set. For example, after you buy the accounts, you may find that one or two of the debtors are deceased or are not property owners. You need time to find these "returns." Three to six months is typical.

You'll be asked to sign a purchase agreement and wire your money to close the deal. The purchase agreement will typically include certain restrictions against reselling the accounts or using the original credit card company's name in any way.

Once you wire your funds, you will be sent a very simple and sparse closing package that includes a Bill of Sale conveying the accounts to you and a spreadsheet listing all of the account information.

As soon as I close on a list of defaulted credit card accounts, I immediately check for bankruptcy filings and then start the collection process. This is where your attorney comes in. I am an attorney and have the advantage of my law firm doing the work "in house." If you are not an attorney, then you will have to retain an attorney and/or a collection agent.

Collection Process

Each state has different local collection laws and rules. Many books have been written on collection lawsuits and the Fair Debt Collection Act, which imposes strict rules on collecting consumer debt. These rules go far beyond what I can cover here. I suggest that unless you are an experienced collection lawyer, you should hire one and rely on his or her expertise. You should focus your time developing an expertise in screening, negotiating, and buying the right accounts.

Attorneys and collection agents usually work on a contingency fee of about one-third of what they collect. You pay all costs such as filing and court fees, and they take one-third off of the top of any funds that they collect. The fee is negotiable, but keep in mind that if you negotiate the fee down, the attorney or collection agent my not have the incentive to work your files quite as hard.

Because the accounts are all seconds and thirds, they have already been "worked" by at least one prior collection agency. They have already been hit with many calls and letters, so don't assume that the debtor will immediately respond to your first letter. In my experience, by the time accounts are sold to a local investor, the debtors have been conditioned to ignore the collection letters. They are used to getting a flurry of letters from time to time, but then nothing happens. My approach is to send the required pre-lawsuit letter and then file a collection lawsuit. Of the hundreds of accounts that I have purchased, only about 5 percent "contested" or opposed my collection lawsuit. Most debtors know they owe the debt and don't want to go to court to fight about it. The overwhelming majority of my collection lawsuits resulted in *unopposed default judgments*.

I then immediately docket the judgment as a lien on the debtor's real estate, and my chances of eventually collecting the debt improves dramatically. Check with your local collection attorney to confirm whether or not judgments can be filed as liens on the debtor's real estate in your state.

Priority & Equity Issues

Once the unsecured credit card debt is converted into a lien through a collection law-suit, the remaining issue is one of *priority and equity*. The lien does not help much if the property is financially underwater. Liens for a money judgment have priority based on the time that they are recorded—*first in time, first in right*. So when you obtain a judgment lien, it will have lower priority than the mortgage and any other judgment liens that have already been filed against the debtor's property. This is no problem if the property is worth more than all of the liens combined, but if there are preexisting higher-priority liens on that property that exceed the property value, then your lien would be considered underwater, or undersecured, and it is much harder to collect.

$200,000 Property Value With Sufficient Equity		$200,000 Property Value "Underwater" Lien with Insufficient Equity	
1st Priority Mortgage:	$150,000	1st Priority Mortgage:	$150,000
2nd Mortgage	$ 20,000	2nd Mortgage	$ 30,000
2014 Judgment Lien:	$ 10,000	2014 Judgment Lien:	$ 20,000
Your New Judgment Lien	$ 10,000	Your New Judgment Lien	$ 10,000
	$ 10,000		$ -10,000

In the first example on the left, there is sufficient equity because all of the liens on the property add up to less than the property value of $200,000. Even though your new judgment lien is lowest priority—after all of the other liens—it is still fully secured because there is enough property value to cover all of the liens.

In the example on the right, there is no equity left over to secure your new judgment lien, because the older, higher-priority liens total $210,000, which is $10,000 more than the value of the property.

Keep in mind that equity coverage changes over time if the property value changes, or if the amount of the other liens change. For example, if the real estate market strengthens, and the property value increases to $220,000, then all of the lien holders would be in a better position. Similarly, if the first mortgage is paid down to $130,000, then the lien holders would be more secure. A lien may start out as undersecured but may become fully secured with sufficient equity if the property value increases and/or the balance of the other liens are reduced through payments.

Collecting on Your Judgment

Congratulations! You just obtained a judgment and recorded it is a lien. Now comes the hard part—converting that piece of paper into cash. The process to enforce judgments varies state by state, but generally the courts do not help much in getting the debtor to pay off your judgment. It is up to you as the judgment creditor to collect your money. It is critical to work with an experienced collection attorney or collection agency; your job is to just monitor their progress to ensure that your files are being worked. Ask for a detailed schedule of the collection steps that they intend to take, along with a time line. The procedures and timing may differ, but in New Jersey it would look something like this:

Activity	Days after File Is Opened
Send demand letter advising of intent to file suit:	5
File collection lawsuit:	40
Obtain default judgment or trial date if opposed:	100

Once judgment is entered, then the collection process starts. Generally, it is a process of trying to get the debtor to engage in a negotiation to pay off the debt. It can include phone calls, letters, and information subpoenas that direct the debtor to list all assets and income sources.

If you find any assets or sources of income, such as a salary, then your attorney or collection agent will arrange to "levy" upon the funds, asset, or wages to pay off your judgment.

Activity	Days after File Is Opened
Phone calls to debtor	as necessary
Mail judgment and information subpoena	5
File motion to enforce subpoena	45
Apply to levy upon any assets or income	as assets & income are discovered

Some states allow for a sheriff's sale of the debtor's real estate under certain circumstances if you have exhausted efforts to collect from less intrusive means. Check with your attorney to see if this is permitted in your state. Unfortunately, judgment liens are low priority, after any other liens that have previously been recorded. The debtor's property is usually encumbered by a mortgage and possibly tax liens and other judgment liens, so there may not be any equity in the property to satisfy your judgment lien.

"Problem-Solving" Approach

In my experience, it is best to take a patient, friendly, problem-solving approach, both with the debtors and with your professionals. Attorneys and collection agents don't like being pressed or being held to a strict time line. If they are good at what they do, they have plenty of other clients and they won't put up with it. You could lose a good member of your professional "team" by pushing too hard. If you are working with the right people, you won't have to harass them to get results. Of course, you should track their progress and make sure a file is not falling through the cracks, but if you are working with the right people, you should not have to micromanage the files for them. If you are not satisfied with your results, you are better off just moving on to a different attorney or collection agency.

When searching for a good collection attorney or collection agency, find out whether they have the required experience and specialization:

1. How long have you been in collections?
2. How many active collection files do you have now?
3. What is your average time line for collecting an account?
4. What is your overall collection percentage rate?

Ask for references and, if possible, try to get the reference into a casual conversation rather than just answering specific questions. Anyone who provides references obviously only will refer people who will give a glowing report, so the key is to get them talking in a relaxed, expansive way if you can. Try to get them to share their experience in general with investing in debt, then work your way to the details about the reference. Find out:

1. How long they have worked with this attorney or collection agency.
2. How many files they have referred to this attorney or collection agency.
3. What percentage they recovered.
4. How long the collection process took.
5. What the best and worst part about working with this attorney or collection agency is.

The same goes for the debtors. Always treat them as you would want a creditor to treat you or a close member of your family. Be reasonable and treat everyone with respect. Bill Bartmann made a fortune buying and collecting consumer debt, and he wrote an excellent book on his collection processes called *Bailout Riches!* I consider it *required reading* for anyone who buys distressed debt. Mr. Bartmann explains that he considers his debtors to be his customers, and he goes into great detail on the collection process that he created through years of trial and error. He stresses repeatedly throughout his book that the best way to succeed in this business is to treat the debtors with the highest respect and with a reasonable problem-solving approach. A quick discounted settlement is always best. It is best to reach a settlement that the debtor can live with—and generates a tidy profit for you, even if you leave a few dollars on the table. Pushing for the maximum possible settlement payment plans is not good business because it usually leads to defaults.

Settlements

Most investors have their attorney or collection agent handle these negotiations, but it is a critical part of this business, so I'll share my view on how to reach successful settlements. Your team of professionals may ask you for your business model on settlements and payment plans, so give it some thought and be prepared to discuss your personal settlement parameters.

The best settlement is a single lump-sum payment that closes the file and allows you to redeploy your funds into the next investment. In my experience, about one-third settled this way, usually at a discount to the amount due, but far more than what I had paid. There are many factors that weigh into this. Large debts are obviously harder to collect in a single lump sum, because most debtors just can't raise a large sum in one shot. It is far easier for a debtor to borrow or scrape together $1,000 or $2,000 to settle a judgment than it is to raise $10,000.

The economy also plays a big role. When I started in this business in 2005, property values were rising and banks were eager to make loans even when the borrower had a poor credit history. The result was that many of my debtors were able to refinance and pay off my judgments quickly in one lump sum payment. Rising property values, low interest rates, and easy credit set a great environment for buying distressed debt. Of course, that all changed in late 2007 when the Great Recession hit. Credit dried up quickly. Banks suddenly stopped lending to anyone with a flawed credit report, and of course, all of our debtors have flawed credit histories, because they have at least one judgment against them (***your judgment***) and usually a few more.

Payment Plans

Due to the debtor's flawed credit rating, and tighter lending standards, many settlements can only be reached through a monthly payment plan. Again, most investors will have their attorney or collection agents negotiate payment plans based on your personal settlement parameters. When negotiating a payment plan, try to get as much information as possible about the debtor's financial condition. People are naturally resistant to disclosing their financial details, so don't be frustrated if they hesitate to share many details. Explain that you are trying to structure a plan that both sides can live with.

Here are some factors that I try to explore when discussing any discounted settlement payment or payment plan:

- Monthly income and sources.
- Monthly expenses such as rent, mortgage, and payments of other debts.
- Does the debtor expect to receive any unusual or one-time payments, such as an inheritance, property sale, tax refund, or lawsuit settlement payment?
- Are there any friends or family members who may help make a settlement payment?
- Intend to sell or refinance property soon?

Processing monthly payments can be double-edged sword. Everyone loves to get checks, and it is great to have the monthly cash flow, but the administration can be a drag. Again, most investors use a collection agency or attorney to collect the accounts, so it eliminates the burden, and you just get a check to cash each month. For those of us who administer the payment plans ourselves, it is a lot of record keeping. I track each payment in a database that I use to track each account from start to finish, and also in my accounting software. I prefer Quickbooks, but there are several off-the-shelf software packages.

Time Is on Your Side

Judgment liens last many years. In New Jersey, the liens remain on the debtor's real property for 20 years and then can be extended. I have seen many files that seemed uncollectable due to the debtor's low income and lack of equity in the property, and then the judgment was unexpectedly paid off. Over time, property values tend to rise, income levels improve, and other higher-priority debts get paid down. As Mick Jagger sang, *Time is on your side*. Work your collection process diligently and then set aside (but never forget) the judgments that seem to be uncollectable. You will be pleasantly surprised when a few of them contact you for a pay-off.

What Can Go Wrong?

The biggest concern for debt buyers is compliance with the Fair Debt Collection Act, which imposes strict rules on how consumer debt can be collected. Many books have been written on this issue, and it is far beyond the scope of this chapter. Before taking any action to buy or collect consumer debt, you must consult with a local attorney who is experienced with the Fair Debt Collection Act. The attorney can help to set up your forms and procedures and ensure that you are in compliance.

Bankruptcy is also a major concern. Credit card debt is dischargeable in bankruptcy, which means that after you pay good money to buy an account, the debtor may file bankruptcy and under the right circumstances have the debt discharged—erased, voided, forgiven. This is part of the business and is to be expected. This is one of the reasons that debt buyers buy these accounts for a discount.

Other risks include death of the debtor, foreclosure of the debtor's property by a superior lien holder, or lack of equity in the debtor's property. All of these scenarios are common and make it much harder or even impossible to collect.

Juniors and seniors who share the exact same name also present a problem when we are trying to establish property ownership. We often think that our debtor is a homeowner with equity (indicating a strong ability to repay a debt) and later find that the debtor is actually the homeowner's son who shares the same name but has no income or assets.

Tips from a Pro

Steve Ruderman has been in the financial services arena for over 30 years and runs *Credit and Collection News*, a daily newsletter specifically designed for the credit and collections marketplace with over 50,000 subscribers. Besides the newsletter, *CCN* also hosts some major industry conferences.

Steve's newsletter is *the* best source of news and resources for debt buyers. Here is Steve's insight on the history and present condition of the market:

> Thirty-five years ago—debt buying was not a concept that was well known or practiced in the credit and collection world. The concept of selling charged-off debt was foreign and unknown. But a few companies like West Capital

went into the business trying to see if there was value to the old debts sitting out there. Boxes of files were sitting in basements with credit grantors gathering dust—so imagine their excitement when debt-buying companies began to approach creditors offering fractions of cents for old charged-off debt. Suddenly that old debt was worth something. Companies would offer creditors dollars for charge-offs and then try and collect on it. The debt was outside the statute of limitations and perceived to have no value. Creditors were quick to sell off these assets to the highest bidders. As the business boomed—so did the prices.

As the new debt-buying industry grew—so did issues and complications. The rules for the industry needed to be updated for this new business. Products and services needed to be redesigned for very old out-of-statute debt. Collectors needed to be retrained on how to collect on the debt. And what happens to interest, negotiation, settling, and even credit reporting? Like any new industry there were lots of growing pains and lots of opportunities. Debt buying became a great way to make money. Buy debts, work them, and then resell the debt to someone else. One company, Commercial Financial Services Inc, emerged as a huge player in the industry. This company run by Bill Bartmann grew to such large extent that Goldman Sachs offered to buy a 20 percent stake in the company and Norwest Bank offered to acquire, but Bartmann refused both offers. Soon the house of cards that CFS built collapsed under the pressure to buy more loans to make a profit and fell into bankruptcy. The industry went from huge opportunity to the bottom. As with any industry—the smaller players took the brunt of the collapse in the industry. Suddenly buyers were stuck with debt they could not collect on.

As the industry righted itself—players like Encore Capital and Portfolio Recovery emerged as legit businesses, complying with the rules and regs of the industry and how to succeed and be a part of the debt cycle. Today there are hundreds of debt-buying companies in the industry both large and small doing very well in the debt-buying market place. They follow both federal and state rules on how to collect on old debts. Technology helps these companies work efficiently in collecting these outstanding debts. Overall the industry has settled into a continued process of the debt-management lifecycle. Federal and state regulatory agencies (like the FTC, CFPB, and State Attorneys General) are constantly monitoring the debt-buying industry, making sure companies comply with state and federal laws designed to protect consumers. The industry has also become a player in regulating itself—creating an association (DBA International) to help maintain a healthy industry for both debt buyers, creditors, and consumers. Debt buying has evolved to a point where credit grantors adapt debt sales as part (or not) of their collection strategy—a much different world than it was 35 years ago.

Steve Ruderman, President
CreditAndCollectionNews.com

Summary of the Pros & Cons

Pros

- ✓ **High Potential Return:** Debt is purchased at deep discounts, so there is great potential upside.
- ✓ **Diversity:** Investment in consumer loans provides a hedge against other investment asset classes such stock or bonds.
- ✓ **Control:** Investors manage risk and income through selection of debt portfolios based on preset criteria and presale due diligence.
- ✓ **Spreading Risk:** Investors may diversify with many debt accounts loans at low values to spread the risk of default.
- ✓ **Outsourcing Work:** Investors typically work with experienced collection attorneys and collection agents to outsource the labor and take advantage of experienced professionals.
- ✓ **Time, Funds, & Expertise:** Unlike many of the investment options discussed in this book, buying credit card debt does not require a lot of time, money, or experience. Investors can start with just $5,000 and rely heavily on a team of professionals.
- ✓ **Scalability:** It is possible to scale up this investment from $5,000 into the millions of dollars once a team of collection professions is in place to perform the work.
- ✓ **Cash Flow:** Settlement payment plans generate cash flow.
- ✓ **Stability:** No "market swings" like the stock market or mutual funds, but economic changes will effect collections.
- ✓ **Professional Assistance:** There are many seasoned collection attorneys and collection agencies to choose from.

Cons

✓ **Fair Debt Collection Act Liability:** Debt buyers are subject to the FDCA and may be fined for violations in collection practices.

✓ **Uncollectable Debt:** Unlike a bank deposit or bank CD, these debt accounts are not FDIC-insured. There is no guarantee of repayment. A portion of the accounts that are purchased will be uncollectible.

✓ **Unpredictable Cash Flow.** Settlement payment plans create a monthly cash flow, but it fluctuates because debtors often miss settlement payments.

✓ **Illiquid:** This is a long-term investment. The collection process is long, and it can take years to collect payments. Although there is a secondary market to resell judgments, it is subject to demand from other investors.

✓ **Fees:** Attorneys and collection agencies generally charge one-third of all funds collected.

✓ **Restrictions:** There are local state restrictions on buying or collecting debt, and investors must be financially qualified or accredited.

✓ **Security & Priority:** Credit card debt is unsecured and low priority in collection efforts. They may be eliminated through bankruptcy and are behind all other secured debt such as mortgages and tax liens.

Hungry for More? Source Books, Consultants, Websites, and Sellers

Debt-Buying Sites:
DBAInternational.org
Kaulkin.com
InsideARM.com
Creditandcollectionnews.com

Books:
Bailout Riches! Bill Bartmann
Invest in Debt, Jim Napier
The Investor's Guide to Buying Debt, Richard L. Shell and John P. Pratt
Collections Made Easy, Carol S. Frischer
Credit Card Nation, Robert D. Manning
A Private Eye's Guide to Collecting a Bad Debt, Fay Faron

4

Defaulted Notes
Buying Defaulted Mortgage Notes

"**SOLD** *to plaintiff for $100!*" Any investor who has sat through a sheriff's sale and watched property after property struck off to the bank has wished they could be the plaintiff. You can. Would you buy a $640,000 mortgage on a condo that appears to be worth about $400,000? The owner still lives there, has not made any mortgage payments or paid condo dues in years. I bought a defaulted note and mortgage just like that. Of course, the price is the key. I paid $280,000. That is a discount of over $100,000 from the property value.

Investors buy defaulted notes and mortgages that are either ready for foreclosure or, better yet, already in the foreclosure process. In buying the note, the investor steps into the shoes of the bank and finishes the foreclosure. If, like in my example above, the debt far exceeds the property value, the eventual sheriff's sale will be struck off to the investor as the plaintiff in the foreclosure action. Then the investor has acquired a distressed property at a discount from the true property value.

The challenges are (1) accurately valuing the property without access to the inside; (2) negotiating a good price for the note and mortgage; (3) efficiently navigating the foreclosure process; and (4) rehabbing and reselling the property.

The risks are relatively high, which is reflected in the price that investors pay. There is often a long foreclosure process during which the property may change value. The debtor may delay the foreclosure and eviction to extend occupancy. The investment is made "As Is" without any access to the interior, so the investor has to make assumptions as to the interior condition of the property.

Possible Scenarios

1. Complete the Foreclosure. The investor forecloses and recaptures the investment funds and profits by reselling the underlying property. This is the intended result. The key is to ensure that the value of the underlying property is sufficiently higher than the amount that you pay for the note, to ensure that you are well secured.

2. Debtor Cures. Debtors have the right to "cure" default and begin making monthly payments to stop a foreclosure. When a debtor cures the default, the note is considered reperforming, and it increases in value. The debtor makes all of the payments required under the note and mortgage, the investor's capital is returned in full, plus the discount (which is the difference between the face value of the note and the discounted price negotiated to buy the note), and the investor earns interest as stated in the note. Not bad. This "curing" or "reperforming" is very unlikely if the note has been in default for years, and especially if the note is "underwater," meaning the amount due far exceeds the property value. Some investors are willing to restructure the note by reducing the interest rate, reducing the monthly payments, or extending the term, to induce the debtor to cure the note.

How Is this Done?

Find Defaulted Notes:

The first step is to find notes to buy. Most mortgages are held by banks and government agencies, and they are not available for assignment. When a debtor falls behind on payments, then the mortgage is considered to be in default ("nonperforming"), and it is treated differently. Federal regulations require banks to mark down the value of the note value for accounting purposes, so the banks have strong incentive to sell them.

Notes can also be purchased from a variety of sources:

- ✓ **Directly from Banks.** Investors can buy directly from a local bank, but banks typically sell their defaulted mortgages in large batches to other banks or large financial companies.
- ✓ **Directly from Private Note Holders.** Investors can search public records for mortgages held by private individuals, which usually occurs when someone sells property and takes back a mortgage as part of the sale proceeds. They often would rather cash out if given the opportunity, especially if a few payments have been missed.
- ✓ **Brokers.** Note brokers can be found on the Internet. They match buyers with sellers who want to assign notes.
- ✓ **Resellers.** Companies buy groups of mortgages and then resell them to smaller investors. I prefer to buy from this source, because I prefer to do repeat business with a known, reputable seller. Investors can find many resellers on the Internet, including Kondaur Capital, Fciexchange.com and Notesdirect.com.

A list of resources for contacting note sellers and brokers is included at the end of this chapter. It is critical to work only with reputable sellers. Regardless of how attractive a deal may appear, I only buy from well-known dealers in the industry. I'd rather pass on a deal than to buy from an unreliable source.

The first step is to get a list of mortgage notes that are being offered for sale. The seller will need some basic information about you and about the type of notes that you are looking for. You will have to qualify as a buyer by signing a nondisclosure agreement.

Always confirm whether the seller is a broker or the actual owner of the notes. Either way is acceptable, but before you begin to negotiate, it is best to know whether you are dealing with a seller or a middleman/broker.

Then the seller will want to know the type of mortgage notes that you are seeking:

- Defaulted, Performing, or Reperforming? "Defaulted" or "nonperforming" means the debtor has stopped making payments. "Performing" means the debtor is making monthly payments and has not defaulted. A "reperforming" or "cured" note had been in default, but the debtor has made a deal to reinstate the loan and is currently making payments.
- State and County? What state or counties are you interested in?
- First Priority? Are you only interested in first-priority loans, or would you buy lower-priority 2nds mortgages?
- Purchase Size? How much money are you willing to invest in a note?

Based on these criteria, the seller will send you a list of notes that are available for you to buy. The list will typically include:

- Property address
- Current balance due
- Date of last payment made
- Property type—single family, multifamily, commercial, or vacant lot
- Owner occupied, leased, or vacant
- Priority of the loan—first or second mortgage

Establishing Property Value

The vast majority of foreclosures are underwater, meaning the lien is greater than the property value, so there is no room for a "White Knight Rescue," as discussed in Chapter Seven. The goal here is to buy the note for considerably less than the property value. The amount due on the note does not matter very much. If you make an offer to buy a note, the offer will be based on what you believe the property is worth.

Like many of the other investments discussed in this book, you must determine the "as is" current value of the property. Most investors work with a local Realtor who can quickly provide a Broker's Price Opinion ("BPO") for the property value. If you don't work with a Realtor, you can compare recent sales data from online Multiple Listing Services to generate your own valuation.

Investors also use free online property research sites, like Zillow.com, Redfin.com, Propertyshark.com, and Trulio.com to gain some insight as to the property value. Just type the address into a search engine, and you will find loads of information about the property. If the property was recently listed for sale, you will be able to find many details and even photos of the interior on real estate listing sites. Like everything else on the Internet, you must be skeptical of what you see. Just because some unknown person posted information about a property does NOT mean it is true. Internet sites are highly valuable tools, but successful investors always confirm the posted information, physically visit the property, and consult with a local broker.

Property Condition and Estimated Costs of Repairs

Your estimated property value will have to include some assumptions. What repairs and improvements will you have to undertake in order to sell the property? How are the roof, the windows, the landscaping? Investors normally cannot get inside the property, so we make assumptions about what will have to be done inside. Properties in foreclosure are usually in distressed condition and often need fresh paint, and updated kitchens and bathrooms. When estimating repair costs, always err on the side of caution and build in a cushion for unexpected repairs. In my experience, there is ALWAYS a surprise or two.

Any Other Liens?

Once you have established a current "as is" property value, you need to determine if there are any higher-priority liens on the property. The seller will advise you whether the loan is a first or second mortgage, but it is up to your own due diligence to find any higher-priority tax liens on the property. If there are open tax liens, you need to find the payoff or "redemption value" of the lien or liens, because you will eventually have to pay the tax liens off. This cost must be factored into the price that you are willing to pay for the note:

Property Value As Is:	$250,000
Pay-off Value of 1st Priority Tax Lien:	-$ 25,000
Net Property Value:	$ 225,000

The seller will advise you whether the note is first priority, but I always get a full title search to verify before I close any deal.

Negotiating a Deal

Resellers are large financial companies that buy notes in bulk packages all over the country. At any given moment, they have several hundred or even thousands of notes in their portfolio. They usually try to add value to their notes by contacting the debtor and trying to get the debtor to start making payments again so the note will be re-labeled as "cured" or "reperforming" which carries a higher value. After they make a limited effort to convert the loans into reperforming, they try to sell off the "fall-out" loans to local investors.

Of course, they want to get the highest price possible, but they typically resell first-priority notes for 40 percent to 60 percent of the underlying property value. Like any other real estate deal, there are many factors that each side can argue to justify a higher or lower price. These acronyms are commonly thrown around:

NPL	Nonperforming loans
UPV	Underlying property value
LTV	Lien-to-value ratio

I like to start negotiations with the "as is" property value ("UPV") because if you can't agree on a general range for the underlying property valuation, you probably won't be able to make a deal. Perhaps one of you has missed an important fact that will change the other's valuation. For example, the seller's information is often stale, and you may know that the property was recently abandoned or damaged. A negotiation on value gives each side the opportunity to share and compare information.

Of course, you don't have to reach an agreement on an exact value. Negotiations always include some "gamesmanship," so both sides are expected to oversell their position to some extent. The goal is just to determine a valuation range, to see if you are both on the "same page." If the seller believes a house is worth $300,000 and you are convinced it is worth $200,000, you are both probably wasting your time.

Once a valuation range is agreed upon, then the negotiations turn to a final price for the mortgage and note. Like any negotiation, there is typically a back-and-forth, with each side offering factors and arguments in support. Keep in mind that the property value has already been negotiated, so at this stage the factors relate more to the steps that the buyer will have to undertake to get possession of the property:

- Has foreclosure been started? If so, how far along?
- Has the owner offered a deed in lieu of foreclosure?
- Is the property more or less likely to be damaged during the foreclosure process?
- What are the terms of the note?
- What does the payment history reveal?

- Is the debtor likely to cure and begin to make payments again?
- What documents are available? The seller must provide you with the original note and mortgage and accurate payment records.

Each of these factors is important in evaluating a potential deal. As you evaluate potential deals, you will find that deals are strong in some factors while weak in others. Some of these factors may be more or less important to you based on your own personal preferences. For example, if your goal is to foreclose and obtain the underlying property, then you'd prefer deals in which the debtor has poor credit, no equity in the property, and a poor payment history with a long period of default. These factors make it very unlikely that the debtor will "cure" and start making payments again.

Conversely, if you'd like to negotiate to convert the note from "nonperforming" into reperforming, these factors will be critical. Be patient and wait for notes that meet your criteria.

Documentation Is Always Critical

Regardless of whether your goal is to foreclose on the note or rework it to get it reperforming, the documentation is always critical. Regardless of how attractive the other aspects of a deal may be, you cannot buy a note unless all of the required documentation is available. The document package varies from state to state, so check with your local attorney; but the seller should at least provide you with the original note, mortgage, payment history, and statement of amount due. The note is absolutely worthless if you lack the documents required to enforce it.

Why It Works

A word on market theory.

So why does this work? Why does this process often result in an investor acquiring a property for less than market value? There are many reasons, but these are the three main factors:

1. **Distressed Property:** Most real estate buyers are not interested in distressed property that needs to be rehabilitated.
2. **Fear of the Unknown:** Of the buyers who are interested in "fixer-uppers," most are scared off by unknown factors that are inherent in navigating through

a foreclosure process. As detailed above, buyers must negotiate without inspecting inside the property.

3. **Capital Requirements:** Investors are required to be accredited investors and must tie up hundreds of thousands of dollars for a long period of time. The purchases cannot be financed, so investors must have fast access to cash.

These factors scare away the vast majority of investors and create a market niche that is far from "perfect." Successful note buyers know how to manage this risk and take advantage of this very "imperfect market" by:

1. Performing due diligence to gather as much information as possible—albeit incomplete;
2. Making rational assumptions about the facts that cannot be discovered; and
3. Maintaining discipline in negotiating the purchase and controlling rehab costs.

Sure, everyone makes mistakes and even the most experienced investor can get burned in this area, but this is a thriving and profitable vehicle for thousands of investors.

Tips from a Pro

Since 1980, Eddie Speed has dedicated his professional life to the nonperforming note industry. Eddie is the owner and president of Colonial Funding Group LLC, which acquires and brokers discounted notes, and he is also a principal in a family of private equity funds that acquires bulk portfolios of notes. Eddie is passionate about teaching others how to succeed in the note business through his NoteSchool.com, a training academy he founded in 2006. He has also opened a site called NotesDirect.com for buyers to shop for notes.

Eddie and his staff offer on line courses, live seminars, and personal mentoring, and I have asked him to provide a few words of wisdom here:

> Since you are reading this, you are at least curious about investing in defaulted notes, and I'd like to encourage you to continue to explore this opportunity. As Mike explains in this book, the most successful investors think "outside the box" and invest a portion of their portfolio in alternative investments that are overlooked by most investors. Buying

defaulted notes is a perfect fit for investors who are willing to do some extra work to make some extra profit.

Mike has already covered the "nuts & bolts" of how to buy notes, so I'll share some insight into the human side of this investment. Always keep in mind that there is a debtor/owner who is directly involved. Most new investors think they have to be cold-hearted toward the debtor, but in my thirty-five years of doing this, I've found the opposite to be true. The most successful note buyers try to work with the debtor.

This can be done in different ways. The first option should always be to see if the note can be made "reperforming." Since you bought the note at a discount, it can be very profitable to restructure it, with lower monthly payments, or a longer term.

If a deal just cannot be worked out, then explore the possibility of a "cash-for-keys" exchange to shorten or eliminate the foreclosure process, and gain possession quickly and inexpensively. Many debtors are looking for a way out and welcome an offer of a few thousand dollars to get started in a new location. This is a win-win solution and can leave both the debtor and the investor feeling good about the deal. Another option is a "deed and lease back," in which the debtor stays in possession as a tenant and pays you rent. If you are open-minded and creative, there are unlimited ways to make money in this field.

—Eddie Speed

What Can Go Wrong

Valuation Errors. The biggest risk in this investment is human error. The key is to (1) obtain an accurate valuation of the property and (2) accurately determine all liens on the property that you will have to pay off. In order to estimate property value, you have to recognize problems with the property and estimate the costs of repairs. Leaking oil tanks, wet lands, zoning issues, and structural issues will severely reduce a property value. Beware of blighted areas with multiple boarded-up houses because it is very difficult to sell property in these areas, so the property values are severely depressed. These risks are common for all of the investment vehicles discussed in this book.

Foreclosure Delays. The foreclosure process can take years. Check with a local foreclosure attorney to gain a full understanding of the timeline and risks in your state. Sheriff's sales and evictions can also be delayed for months. Factor a "worst case scenario" into your offer.

Bankruptcy. Bankruptcy is also a common setback, and it is an unavoidable risk in this business. A bankruptcy will delay foreclosure, but the mortgage lien will not be eliminated. A debtor's bankruptcy can usually be dismissed if the debtor fails to pay current mortgage and property taxes. If you buy notes that are "underwater" (more than the property is worth), bankruptcy is less of an issue.

Documentation. Order a full title search before you buy any note, to ensure that the mortgage is recorded in the name of the seller and has not been foreclosed out already by a higher-priority lien holder. Be sure to get the full loan package because a note is not legally enforceable without the proper documents. The document package varies from state to state, so check with your local attorney.

The three most common pitfalls are *title, tax liens*, and *blight*. Your title search should confirm that the seller properly holds the note. You would not want to buy a note from an entity that does not hold that note, right? Tax liens should be discovered through a title search, as well. Tax liens have higher priority and must be paid off, so you must determine the cost of any tax liens before you close your deal. Blighted or severely depressed neighborhoods should be avoided.

These risks are the reasons that investors are able to buy notes at deep discounts to the property value. If there were no risks, then there would be no reward. If these risks are not for you, then don't invest in this area.

Summary of the Pros & Cons

Pros

- ✓ **High potential return:** Potential profit is comparably high.
- ✓ **Diversity:** Investment in real estate provides a hedge against other investment asset classes such as stock or bonds.
- ✓ **Security & Priority:** These notes are secured and can be first priority so they are ahead of other secured debt such as second mortgages and judgment liens.
- ✓ **Control:** Investors manage risk through individual selection of notes.
- ✓ **Scalability:** There are plenty of opportunities, if your financing allows for multiple purchases.
- ✓ **Stability:** No "market swings" like the stock market or mutual funds.

Cons

- ✓ **Foreclosure Delays:** The foreclosure process takes many months and can be delayed, which increases costs and delays the return of capital.
- ✓ **Bankruptcy Delays:** Debtors may file bankruptcy to delay the foreclosure process, but the mortgage lien is not eliminated or discharged as long as there is equity in the property.
- ✓ **Property Rehabilitation Costs:** Foreclosed properties usually require renovation and repairs before the property can be sold. These repairs can be costly and time-consuming.
- ✓ **Illiquid:** This is a long-term investment due to the foreclosure process.
- ✓ **Capital requirements:** The cost of buying notes and repairing the property is usually over $100,000.

Hungry for More? Source Books, Consultants, Websites, and Sellers

Note-buying sites:
www.noteschool.com
www.notesdirect.com
www.fciexchange.com

Books:
Fast Cash, How I Made a Fortune Buying Notes, Lorelei Stevens
Private Mortgage Investing, Teri B. Clark & Matthew Stewart Tabacchi

5

Performing Notes
Buying Mortgage Notes at a Discount

L ooking for cash flow secured by a lien on real property? This chapter is similar to the previous chapter on investing in defaulted notes, but there are a few major differences. When you buy a *defaulted* mortgage, there are two options. You can try to negotiate with the debtor to restructure the debt and convert the loan from "nonperforming into "reperforming." If that is not possible, then the goal is to acquire the underlying real estate. When you buy a ***performing*** mortgage, on the other hand, the loan is not in default, so the goal is to acquire a secured stream of income at a discount.

These are long-term deals with less turnover of your money. The model is to buy a note and hold it for years as it is paid off through monthly payments. Investors are attracted to the cash flow, which is secured by a lien and acquired at a discounted price. These performing mortgages attract a different type of investor from defaulted notes, which are purchased with the goal of making a large capital gain, rather than a long-term income stream.

The challenges are (1) accurately valuing the property without access to the inside; (2) negotiating a good price for the note and mortgage; and (3) collecting and administering the monthly payments from the debtor.

The main risk is default by the debtor, but the risk is reduced if the loan is purchased for a good discounted price. The key is to perform proper due diligence to ensure that the underlying property value is significantly more than the price that you pay for the note. There is no set or standard price for these notes. The price can be based on a discount from the amount due on the note, or on a discount from the value of the underlying property. Either way, you pay less than the amount due on the note.

Notes with a small balance due, secured by higher-value property are typically priced based on a percentage of the amount due on the note, because the note is well secured by the high property value. For example, a $10,000 note secured by a $200,000 property would be priced based on a discount from the amount due on the note.

Larger notes that are close to (or exceeding) the value of the underlying property are priced based on a percentage of the property value. Investors typically pay anywhere from 60 to 90 percent of the property value depending on several factors discussed in detail below.

The investment is made "as is," often without any access to the interior, so the investor has to make assumptions as to the interior condition of the property.

Possible Scenarios

1. *Debtor makes required payments.* If the debtor does not default, and makes all of the payments required under the note and mortgage, the investor's capital is returned in full, plus the discount (which is the difference between the face value of the note and the discounted price negotiated to buy the note), and the investor earns interest as stated in the note. Not bad.

2. ***Debtor pays off early.*** Many debtors refinance or sell the property, which triggers an early payoff. Again, the investor's capital is returned in full, plus the discount, and the investor earns interest as stated in the note. The bonus here is that your capital and the discount are returned faster than expected.

3. ***Debtor defaults.*** If the debtor stops making the payments as required in the note, this investment model converts over to the previous chapter on investing in defaulted notes. First try to "work out" the loan to get the debtor to make payments again, and if a deal cannot be worked out, you must foreclose and recapture the investment funds by reselling the underlying property. This is not the intended result, but it is a common occurrence, so investors must plan for this potential outcome when negotiating to buy the note. The key is to be certain that the value of the underlying property is sufficiently higher than the amount that you pay for the note, to ensure that you are well secured.

How is This Done?

Find Performing Notes

Finding and buying performing notes is similar to the process as described in the previous chapter on defaulted notes. A list of resources for contacting note sellers and brokers is included at the end of this book. Sources include:

- Directly from banks
- Directly from private note holders
- Brokers
- Resellers
- Running ads in CraigsList.com or newspapers

The process is the same as buying a defaulted note, but the pricing is different for a performing note. Nonperforming, defaulted notes are priced at a discount to the value of the underlying property, with adjustments for the anticipated foreclosure process. Performing notes, on the other hand, are priced based on the anticipated future income from monthly payments. The discount varies based on many factors, including:

- Priority of the note—first or second priority mortgage
- Past defaults
- Level of equity to secure the loan

- Credit score of the debtor
- Term (length) of the note
- Documentation of the debt and payment history
- Time since last default ("seasoning")
- Balance due
- Lien to value ratio

Just like when buying a defaulted note, the seller will provide a list that typically includes:

- Property address
- Current balance due
- Date of last payment made
- Property type—single family, multifamily, commercial, or vacant lot
- Owner-occupied, leased, or vacant
- Priority—first or second mortgage
- Payment & default history
- Documentation of the loan

Reviewing the "Tape" of Notes For Sale

Here is an example of what a typical list of notes or "tape" would include:

View Details	State	Description	Lien	Type	Class	Price	UPB%	Rate	YTM	LTV
View Details	TX	Performing serviced note, 11% yield, Texas	1st	Residential	Loans to Sell	$65.7k	88%	8%	18%	77%
View Details	TX	6 month payments, performing serviced note, 11% yield, Texas	1st	Residential	Loans to Sell	$55.3k	89%	8%	18%	74%
View Details	SC	Note for sale with a 12% Yield!	1st	Residential	Loans to Sell	$69.4k	82%	9%	16%	80%
View Details	CA	65% LTV; Cash-Out Refi of a N/O/O SFR in Lancaster, CA	1st	Residential	Loans to Sell	$126k	100%	8%	N/A	65%
View Details	CA	65% LTV; Purchase of a N/O/O SFR in Oakland, CA	1st	Residential	Loans to Sell	$201k	100%	9%	N/A	65%
View Details	CA	70% LTV; 696 FICO; Purchase of a N/O/O SFR in LA, CA.	1st	Residential	Loans to Sell	$205k	100%	9%	N/A	70%
View Details	CA	64% LTV; 687 FICO; C/O Refi of a N/O/O 4-Plex in Hemet, CA	1st	Residential	Loans to Sell	$169k	100%	9%	N/A	64%
View Details	TX	65% LTV; Cash-Out Refi of a N/O/O SFR in Dallas, TX	1st	Residential	Loans to Sell	$234k	100%	8%	N/A	65%
View Details	CA	59% LTV; 734 FICO; C/O Refi of a SFR in Hollywood Hills, CA	1st	Residential	Loans to Sell	$4M	100%	10%	N/A	59%

By "clicking through" to the details column on the left, more details are revealed about the loan:

General Information

Listing Number: XXX

Listing Type: Basic

Are Broker Inquiries Welcome?: Yes

Broker Points: 1.0

Loan Classification: Loans to Sell

Loan Type: Seller Carryback

Interest Rate: 8.0%

Interest Type: Fixed

Payment Frequency: Monthly

Term: 10

Remaining Term: 9

Balloon: No

Carryback?: No

Lien Position: 1st

Loan Balance: $62,361

Property Details

Asset Type: Residential

Property Type: Single Family

Current Property Value: $74,900

Location

City: Cleveland

State: TX

Region: Southwest

Zip/Postal: 77328

Country: US

Valuation

LTV - Current ?: 73.8%

Last Valuation Date: 9/1/2015

Valuation Source: Other

Selling Price: $55,262

Negotiable?: Yes

UPB%: 88.6%

Recovery Probability: 100%

Yield to Maturity ?: 18.4%

Payment

Payment: $787.42

Performance: Performing

Pay History: A 0x30

Credit Grade: U Unknown

Other

In Foreclosure: No

Reason for Selling: Cash out

The buyer's due diligence is the same as buying a defaulted note:

- Establish the "as is" value of the underlying property
- Determine other liens
- Estimate equity securing the loan

- Review the payment/default history
- Review available documentation of the loan

Advantages of Second Mortgages

Who would want to buy a second mortgage that has lower priority than a larger, first mortgage on the property? It is counterintuitive, but many investors actually refer second mortgages.

Again, the key is to get an accurate valuation of the underlying property, so that you can be sure that there is enough equity in the property to adequately secure the second mortgage:

Property Value As Is:	$300,000
Pay off Value of 1st Priority Tax Lien:	-$ 15,000
Value of First Mortgage:	-$200,000
Value of Second Mortgage:	-$ 25,000
Equity Cushion:	$ 60,000

In this example, there is $60,000 in equity after the first mortgage, tax lien, and second mortgage; so even though the second mortgage is lower priority—behind the tax lien and first mortgage—there is sufficient equity to secure the second mortgage. The amount of equity is the key factor in determining the value of the second mortgage note.

More Equity = More Security = Higher Cost to Buy Note

Assuming there is adequate equity to secure the loan, second mortgages have some clear advantages over firsts:

- **Size.** They are normally much smaller, so it takes less capital, allowing an investor to spread risk among several different notes.
- **Price Discount.** Investors get bigger discounts on second-priority notes, so the payoff is better.
- **Higher Interest Rate.** Second mortgage notes usually carry a higher interest rate than a first mortgage.
- **Often Paid Off Early.** Because the second mortgage is smaller and bears a higher interest rate, debtor often pay them off or refinance them earlier, which means the investor recovers the capital and discount earlier.

The major disadvantage of investing in a second mortgage loan is that there is a large first mortgage ahead of it that has priority over (and can foreclose on) the second mortgage. Because of this lower priority, you must be prepared to pay off the first mortgage if the debtor defaults and the first mortgage goes into foreclosure. Investors must always maintain funds to cover this potential problem.

Again, these acronyms are commonly used in price negotiations:

AR	Adjusted Return on capital
IR	Interest Rate
UPV	Underlying Property Value
LTV	Lien To Value ratio

Just like investing in defaulted notes, I always start negotiations with the "as is" property value ("UPV") because if you can't agree on a general range for the underlying property valuation, then you probably won't be able to make a deal. Once a valuation range is agreed upon, the negotiations turn to a final price for assignment of the note and mortgage. Final negotiations turn to likelihood of a default:

- Has the debtor defaulted on any mortgage? If so, how long ago? Prior defaults are seen as increasing the likelihood of another default.
- What is the amount of equity cushion above all liens?
- Is the property more or less likely to be damaged in the future?
- Is the property area generally increasing or decreasing in value?

Servicing

The term *servicing* refers to collecting, processing, and tracking all of the monthly payments that are made by the debtor under the terms of the note. Large banks hire "servicing" companies to handle this tedious and detailed-oriented work. It is critical to keep accurate records to protect yourself and the debtor. If a note is defaulted and a foreclosure is required, the debtor may demand to see the payment records, and if there are any inaccuracies, it can cause months of costly delays while the attorneys fight it out in court. If you are not the type to keep immaculate records; then use a servicer. In fact, many of the more reputable note sellers will not sell performing notes to you unless you are working with a servicer. Servicers typically charge a small fee of $25 to $40 per month, so it is worth the cost.

Documentation

This is an important aspect that is often overlooked. One would assume that if you are being offered a note to buy, all of the necessary documentation would be in place. Unfortunately, however, it is not always the case. Some unscrupulous sellers will shop notes around "for sale" when they don't even own the note yet. Once they find a potential buyer, then they will scramble to buy it from another seller and "flip" it to you for a profit. Other sellers will try to sell you a note with incomplete documentation.

I only work with a limited number of well-respected sellers whom I can trust. In order to close a deal, you should receive the entire loan package, including:

1. Original promissory note
2. Original recorded mortgage
3. Complete payment records
4. Signed statement of account due
5. Assignment of note and mortgage
6. Legal file if one exists

Before you get too deep into negotiations, be sure to establish whether you are negotiating with a broker or the true holder of the note and determine whether the seller can provide full documentation of the loan. The required documentation varies from state to state, so check with your local attorney to confirm what documents are needed in your region.

Why It Works

A word on market theory.

So why does this work? Why does this process often result in an investor acquiring an income stream that is better than buying a bond or a bank CD? There are many reasons, but there are two main factors:

1. **Fear of the Default:** Most investors seeking an income stream seek safety, so they settle for relatively low-yielding, guaranteed bank CDs, municipal bonds, or mortgage-backed securities. The risk of default scares away most income investors.
2. **Capital Requirements:** Investors must tie up tens of thousands of dollars for a long period of time. The purchases cannot be financed, so investors must have fast access to cash.

These factors scare away the vast majority of income investors and create a market niche for income investors who are willing to take on more risk and who know how to manage the risk to take advantage of this niche market by:

1. Performing good due diligence to determine the equity level and potential risk of default;
2. Make rational assumptions about the facts that cannot be discovered;
3. Maintain discipline in negotiating the purchase and managing collection of monthly payments.

Tips From a Pro

Eddie Speed has been investing in notes for over 30 years. He has taught me a lot, and he shares his experience though his "Note School" business. He has also opened a site called NotesDirect.com for buyers to shop for notes. Eddie and his staff offer online courses, live seminars, and personal mentoring, and I have asked him to provide a few words of wisdom here.

First off, I congratulate you on taking the first step of reading this chapter, and I welcome you to a very profitable business. I have not seen a market this good in over 30 years of investing. There are many opportunities, but, like anything else in life, you MUST know what you are doing or you can lose your shirt.

I tell all of my students that there are basically six categories of any note deal:

1. The Borrower;
2. The Collateral;
3. The Amount of Equity;
4. The Terms of the Note;
5. The Payment History; and
6. The Documentation.

Don't buy any note unless you have a full understanding of the note in each of these categories. Some aspects may be stronger or weaker, but you must do your homework in each of these six areas in order to gain a full understanding of the strengths and weaknesses of the deal. I've seen far too many investors fall in love with one or two aspects of a note and ignore major weaknesses in other areas. For example, no matter how strong the borrower and collateral may be, you should never buy any note if the documentation is not fully available and in order.

Note buyers who remain disciplined, do their homework, and treat the debtors with fairness and respect can do very well in in this business. I welcome you to the club!

What Can Go Wrong

The risks are similar to investing defaulted notes.

Property Valuation Errors. The biggest risk in this investment is human error. The key is to accurately determine the property value and equity level by (1) obtaining an accurate value of the property, and (2) accurately determining all liens on the property that may have higher priority over your loan.

Default & Foreclosure Delays. The foreclosure process can take years. Check with a local foreclosure attorney to gain a full understanding of the timeline and risks in your state. Sheriff's sales and evictions can also be delayed for months. Factor a "worst case scenario" into your offer.

Bankruptcy. Bankruptcy is also a common setback, and it is an unavoidable risk in this business. A bankruptcy will delay foreclosure, but the mortgage lien will not be eliminated. A debtor's bankruptcy can usually be dismissed if the debtor fails to pay current mortgage and property taxes. Be proactive with your attorney to push for payments in the first month after a bankruptcy is filed.

These risks are the reason that investors are able to buy notes at deep discounts. If there were no risks, then there would be no reward. If these risks are not for you, don't invest in this area.

Summary of the Pros & Cons

Pros

✓ **High Return:** Potential profit is comparably high.

✓ **Cash Flow:** Monthly payments provide a nice cash flow.

✓ **Diversity:** Investment in real estate provides a hedge against other investment asset classes such stock or bonds.

✓ **Security & Priority:** These notes are secured by liens on real property.

✓ **Control:** Investors manage risk through individual selection of notes.

✓ **Scalability:** There are plenty of opportunities, if your financing allows for multiple purchases.

✓ **Stability:** No "market swings" like the stock market or mutual funds.

✓ **Liquidity:** This is a long-term investment, but there is an active secondary market for performing notes through note brokers.

Cons

✓ **Default & Foreclosure Delays:** Unlike a bank deposit or bank CD, these loans are not FDIC-insured. There is no guarantee of repayment. Borrowers will default on a percentage of loans, and it will reduce the investor's return.

✓ **Bankruptcy Delays:** Additionally, the grading supplied by Lending Club and Prosper may be inaccurate, underestimating default risks.

✓ **Capital Requirements:** The cost of buying performing a note is usually $25,000 or higher.

Hungry for More? Source Books, Consultants, Websites, and Sellers

Note buying sites:

www.noteschool.com

www.notesdirect.com

Books:

Fast Cash, How I Made a Fortune Buying Notes, Lorelei Stevens

Private Mortgage Investing, Teri B. Clark & Matthew Stewart Tabacchi

6

Sheriff's Sales
Buying Properties at Foreclosure Sales

Buying a foreclosed property at a sheriff's sale is one of the most common ways to invest in distressed property. It is a well-known investment vehicle because it is straightforward and simpler than most of the other investments discussed in this book. This is not an investment in debt *directly*, because you are not really buying debt. Investors are buying real property that is being sold through a debt collection procedure. I have included it in this book anyway, because it is so closely related to purchasing and collecting debt, and it is a great place for investors to start.

Summary Points

1. **Specialized Knowledge:** Property values, searching public records; rehab.
2. **High Capital Requirement:** Purchase prices can be hundreds of thousands of dollars, and it is hard to arrange mortgage financing for a sheriff's sale bid.
3. **Scalability:** Yes; many potential opportunities but requires a lot of time and cash
4. **Liquidity:** Depends on the local property market
5. **Priority over other debt:** Properties can be purchased free and clear of their liens, or subject to higher priority liens.
6. **Barriers to Entry:** Cash required and time-consuming

How This Works

Many debt collection lawsuits, such as mortgage foreclosures, conclude with a sheriff's sale or public auction of property that was posted by the debtor to secure the loan. The property is often referred to as "collateral," "mortgaged property," "underlying property," or "subject property." These foreclosure sales are commonly known as judicial sales or sheriff's sales because the sales are ordered by the court and typically are conducted by the sheriff's department in the county where the property is located. These sales are the final step in a legal proceeding to collect on a debt that is secured by a lien on property. The auctions are advertised to the public in newspapers and on websites, and are open to the public for bidding. The properties that are to be sold are identified in advance so potential investors can determine which (if any) property to bid upon.

Foreclosure sales can result from many different legal proceedings depending on state laws, such as:

- Mortgage foreclosure
- Tax lien foreclosure
- Judgments for money damages
- Government seizures in drug or other criminal cases

Investors who acquire property at foreclosure auctions can acquire real estate at an attractive discount to the market value of the property. Properties are often sold at discounts of 20 percent to 30 percent below the as-is property value.

The procedures and terms vary in different states and counties. For example, in some states, mortgage foreclosures end in a sheriff's sale, and others states use a quicker, nonjudicial foreclosure procedure:

1. *Judicial Sale; Sheriff's Sale; Court Foreclosure:*
   These terms are used in states that have adopted a more formal court procedure to foreclose. This "judicial" process involves filing and serving a complaint, entry of a judgment, and eventually a "writ" or court order directing the county sheriff's department to conduct a sheriff's sale of the subject property. The sales are typically held by a sheriff's officer at the county court house in the county where the property is located, and it results in the issuance of sheriff's deed. This judicial foreclosure process is costlier and slower than the nonjudicial procedure.

2. *Nonjudicial Sale; Deed of Trust; Trustee sales:*
   These terms relate to jurisdictions that utilize a less formal foreclosure process that does not involve the court system. In these states, lenders obtain a "deed

of trust" rather than a mortgage, and they hold a contractual "power of sale" that, upon default, allows the lender to have the property sold by a private sale—with no court proceedings. The sales are held by an appointed trustee after the debtor is provided notice of default and allowed a period of time to cure (pay off). The trustee (who may or may not happen to be a sheriff's officer) advertises and conducts the "trustee's sale" often at the property itself. This nonjudicial foreclosure process is less costly and much faster than judicial foreclosures.

This chapter is intended to provide an introductory overview. Investors who are interested in pursuing this opportunity should look into books that are entirely on this subject, such as Marc Sherby's *How To Buy Real Estate at Foreclosure Auctions* and should check with a local attorney to get details on their local area.

Finding Sales

The process of finding sales has become much easier in recent years. In my home state of New Jersey, all of the county sheriff departments are online, and they list the sales on a free website. Sheriff's sales are also advertised in local newspapers and can be found on foreclosure websites that provide information about pending foreclosures for a fee.

Be careful with these websites. In my experience, many of the "foreclosure lists" that are offered for sale on the Internet are not worth the price because much of the information is inaccurate or stale, and it is all available for free. There are exceptions that are worth the fee, but they are generally regional. For example, RapidTrusteeSale. com compiles and reports on foreclosure sales in California, Arizona, and Nevada, and I understand that this service is generally reliable and cost-efficient. Services such as this collect information on upcoming foreclosure sales by "scraping" public notices from a variety of websites and publications and compiling the information on a single website. Again, these services can help save a lot of time as long as the data are updated and accurate.

As illustrated in the following "Foreclosure Sales Listing" that I copied from a sheriff's department website in New Jersey, the published notice lists provide the date of each scheduled auction, the name of the plaintiff (which is usually a bank or government agency that holds a mortgage), the name of the defendant property owner, and the address of the property to be sold.

Any County, NJ - Foreclosure Sales Listing

Click the Details link next to the property to view additional information. (1254 search results)

	Sheriff #	Sales Date	Plaintiff	Defendant	Address
Details	FOR-140020	5/9/2016	Bayview Loan Servicing	John Doe	1 Maple Ave, Homeville
Details	FOR-140027	5/9/2016	Wells Fargo Bank	Donald Debtor	4 Seeley Ave, Springfield
Details	FOR-140031	5/9/2016	Bayview Loan Servicing	Debbie Debtor	5 County Route 37, Debtorville, NJ
Details	FOR-140040	5/9/2016	Wells Fargo Bank,	Jane Doe	2 Westwood Road Hometown, NJ
Details	FOR-150002	5/9/2016	Deutsche Bank	Vic Vacant	1 Ash St., Farmville NJ

The table above is just an example, and you will find that each county and state may provide the information in a different format, but these basic facts are typically included so that investors can decided whether, and how much, to bid.

Note the "Details" column on the left of the chart above. This link would bring you to some more details, which in this example (below) includes the size of the property, the amount of the debt ("Upset Price"), and the plaintiff's attorney.

"Status history" such as the above table, is also often available on sheriff's sites. This example reveals that the sale has been repeatedly adjourned by the plaintiff. The reason is not provided but could be:

- **Bankruptcy:** Debtors often file bankruptcy just before a sale so the "automatic stay" will stop the sale.
- **Settlement discussions:** If the bank believes that a debtor is close to curing or paying off the loan, the bank will often delay the sale to allow more time to settle.
- **Due diligence:** Banks like to know what they are getting at the sale, so they will often delay a sale if they have not completed their analysis of the property.

Sales Listing Details

Sheriff #:	FOR-150009
Court Case #:	F39363
Sales Date:	5/9/2017
Plaintiff:	Wells Fargo Bank, N.A.
Defendant:	Donald Debtor
Address:	2 Tilton Drive Oceanville NJ
Description:	DIMENSIONS OF LOT: 110.75' x 149.04' NEAREST CROSS STREET: 484' from Green Grove Road SUPERIOR INTERESTS (if any): NONE
Approx. Upset*:	$566,070.73
Attorney:	Pellegrino & Feldstein, LLC

Status History

Status	Date
Adjournment Plaintiff	5/09/2016
Adjournment Plaintiff	4/04/2016
Adjournment Plaintiff	3/07/2016
Adjournment Plaintiff	12/07/2015
Adjournment Plaintiff	10/13/2015
Adjournment Defendant	7/13/2015
Adjournment Plaintiff	6/29/2015
Scheduled	5/26/2015

*Excludes Judgment Interest and Sheriff Fees.

The following is an example of a newspaper publication announcing a sheriff's sale. Notice that the ad identifies the property, provides the location and time of the sale, sets payment terms, and discloses the amount of the judgment, which typically is the "upset price" to which the bank will usually bid.

County: Essex
Printed In: The *Star-Ledger*, Newark

Public Notice

Shaun Golden MONMOUTH COUNTY SHERIFF NOTICE OF FORECLO-
SURE SALE SUPERIOR COURT OF NEW JERSEY MONMOUTH COUNTY
CHANCERY DIVISION Docket No. F-XXX-16 Sheriff's File #XXXXXXX Free-
dom Mortgage Corp, Plaintiffs v John Doe, et al., Defendants By virtue of a writ
of execution in the above stated action to me directed, I shall expose for sale at
public venue, at Hall of Records, 1 East Main Street (2nd Floor—Freeholders
Meeting Room), in the Borough of Freehold, County of Monmouth, New Jersey,
on Monday, the 9th day of September, 2017 at 2 o'clock, P.M. prevailing time.
The property to be sold is located in the Township of Pleasantville in the County
of Monmouth, State of New Jersey. Tax Lot: X Tax Block: Y; Commonly known
as: 124 Mockingbird Lane, Pleasantville, NJ, Approximate dimensions: 571.00' x
40.00' x 210.50' x 100.00' x 210.50' Nearest cross street: Sweetmans Lane. Surplus Money: If after the sale and satisfaction of the mortgage debt, including costs
and expenses, there remains any surplus money, the money will be deposited into
the Superior Court Trust Fund and any person claiming the surplus, or any part
thereof, may file a motion pursuant to Court Rules 4:64–3 and 4:57–2 stating the
nature and extent of that person's claim and asking for an order directing payment
of the surplus money. The Sheriff or other person conducting the sale will have
information regarding the surplus, if any. A full legal description of the premises
can be found in the Office of The Sheriff of Monmouth County. TERMS OF SALE:
DEPOSIT: 20% of the bid amount at the time of sale. Balance due in 30 days. Cash
or certified check only. The approximate amount of the judgment, Commission and
costs to be satisfied by sale is the sum of $440,341.58. The successful bidder will be
responsible for all fees, commissions and costs of sale. The Sheriff hereby reserves
the right to adjourn this sale without further notice by publication. Shaun Golden,
Sheriff Dated: 8/14/2013, 8/21/2013, 8/28/2013, 9/4/2013, Attorney, for the firm
[NJ Law Firm listed here]

Public Notice ID: XYZ123

Due Diligence

Due diligence is the presale research that investors undertake before they bid on a property. The ultimate goal is to determine what the property is worth in its current condition, so the investor can make an informed decision as to how high to bid.

This is the biggest challenge. Properties are obviously sold "as is," so bidders take the risk as to the condition and value of the property. Bidders gather as much information as possible, make assumptions as to what can't be determined, and then set a maximum bid based on the "worst case scenario."

The ultimate goal is to determine a maximum bid for the property in its current condition. The best way to do that is to "back into it" by estimating the sale value of the property after it is fixed up for resale, and then subtracting how much it would cost to get the property into that resale condition. In order to calculate the maximum bid, an investor must estimate four values:

- What will the property be worth after it is fixed up and resold? To do this, we compare resent sale prices of similar properties.
- What is the cost of the repairs?
- What will the carrying and resale costs be? This includes cost of funds (interest), insurance, property taxes, utilities, condo fees (if applicable), recording fees, inspection fees, attorney fees, and Realtor commissions.
- What will be the cost of paying off any superior liens that will remain on the property after it is purchased?

Estimating the Resale Value

Potential bidders normally are not permitted to enter a property that is listed for a sheriff's sale, so there is a fair amount of guesswork and estimations that must be made. Faced with this restriction, investors have found other means to try to pin down a value.

Experienced investors do an initial quick screening to eliminate any properties that are obviously worth less than the bank's upset price if known. No sense spending more time completing a diligent review on a property that will clearly be struck off back to the bank for the amount of the mortgage. Many foreclosed properties are worth less than the amount of the mortgage, so it is common for the property to be sold to the bank for its upset price.

In determining a resale value, we compare the subject property to other similar properties that have recently been sold. In order to make an accurate comparison, we need to determine as many factors as possible, including:

- Type and style of property. Is it residential or commercial? Which style? Colonial, Tudor, Cape Cod, Victorian?
- Number of bedrooms and bathrooms?
- Age of building?
- Square footage?
- Location?
- Occupied or vacant?

To avoid missing anything, most investors make a check list to evaluate every aspect of a property. ***Use the Property Due Diligence Checklist included in the Appendix at the end of this book.***

This may seem obvious to some, but investors should drive by and ***personally*** look at the target property as part of the due diligence process. Bidders attending auctions will run into helpful people who will offer to provide "due diligence" reports that summarize all available data about a property before an auction. I have no problem with these services, but I would never bid on any property unless I took at least a quick look myself.

Personally inspecting a property provides the best feel for the condition of the house and the neighborhood. Take photos of the property and the neighborhood. Chatty neighbors often strike up conversations about the property and sometimes offer useful information, like how long the property has been vacant or whether the basement floods every fall.

I have seen many people make costly mistakes in this presale due diligence. It is critical to be sure of what you are bidding upon. For example, it is often difficult to determine exactly which property is being sold. The published listing includes the street address and the block and lot number, so it would seem to be easy to find the house, but distressed houses often do not have house numbers on them. The block and lot number is not physically listed on the property, so it can be tricky to determine exactly which property is being sold. As I write this chapter, I have a client who bought a sliver of a vacant lot, when he thought he was bidding on the house next door. Check the lot dimensions on the tax map to confirm that the size matches the property that you are looking at.

Online Data

Thankfully, more and more information is available online, and investors can use these free and easy resources to learn about a property before bidding:

- County records such as tax assessments, which often include the prior sale price.
- Realtor Multiple Listing ("MLS") sites reveal property values of similar properties in the neighborhood. Many properties that are up for sheriff's sale are currently, or were recently, listed for sale through a Realtor, so the MLS will include loads of details about the property, including interior photos.
- Real estate sites such as Zillow, Trulia, Redfin, and Property Shark include valuable information, but it is not always accurate.

Realtors

A local Realtor can be an investor's best asset, but be skeptical. Through years of trial and error, I have been fortunate to build a team of Realtors who really know their local market and understand the business of rehabbing and reselling property. They can make this investment much easier, and they maximize profits. Like any professionals, however, Realtors vary greatly in their ability. Some are part-timers who pick up a Realtor's license later in life, more as a hobby than a career. I have dealt with many who have very limited experience and offer no value other than to print lists from the Multiple Listing directory. Some seem to be entirely motivated by their own commissions, so they recommend *every* deal and exhibit no appreciation for the ultimate goal of turning a fair profit. Watch for Realtors who give you high valuations before you invest and then suggest lower listing prices after you have acquired the property and need to resell it. Also, be skeptical of Realtors who push for expensive upgrades that will help to sell the property quickly. Of course, we all want a quick sale, but each expense must be calculated to increase your profit. It doesn't make sense to make expensive upgrades that will not add to the bottom line.

Again, I mean no disrespect to real estate agents in general. Just be careful to build the right team with Realtors who understand this investment model and who put your interests ahead of their own desire to turn a quick commission.

Most new investors prefer to start with single-family houses as opposed to vacant land or commercial properties. Single-family houses (SFH) are plentiful and usually have a lower cost than commercial properties. Vacant land can be very tricky to value because it is often difficult to assess whether a lot is buildable. What are the zoning restrictions? Can a septic system be installed? Is there an active market to resell lots in the neighborhood?

Investors typically favor properties that are close to home for a few reasons. It is easier to keep an eye on them and to rehab properties that are close. Investors also tend to be more familiar with property values and trends in their neighborhood and already know local contractors.

Estimating the Repair / Rehab Costs

Curbside Inspections: Bidders visually inspect properties without trespassing onto the property. From these quick "drive-by" inspections, a bidder can get a general appraisal of the overall condition of the property and the neighborhood. The external condition usually reflects the interior condition, as well. If the exterior of a house is in poor shape, you can certainly assume the interior also has not been maintained. An investor can make a quick and free evaluation simply by eyeballing a few factors.

What does the structure look like?

- Occupied or vacant?
- Underground oil tank is a negative factor. Can you spot a heating oil filling spout, or a gas service meter?
- Roof condition? Need to be replaced? Just patched?
- Windows: broken, old single pane?
- Siding: Type and condition?
- Pool? Pools are disfavored by most buyers.
- Off-street parking? Driveway and garage?
- Landscaping?
- Condition of neighboring homes?

Bidders are not permitted to trespass onto the property, but it is not uncommon for bidders to take a quick peek into the windows of an abandoned house. This is not recommended for occupied houses for obvious reasons.

Assume the worst. Many details about the condition of the property often cannot be determined, so we must assume the worst. If the kitchen, bathroom, heating, and cooling systems cannot be evaluated, then most investors will assume that they must be replaced. This assumption rule can create a big advantage for an investor who can get more information than the other bidders. If everyone else is bidding based on an assumption that at the interior is a mess, and one bidder has confirmed that the interior is actually in decent shape, that informed bidder can safely outbid the others and win the property. One of my clients knocks on the door and offers $50 to inspect the house for five minutes. He has a lot of guts and is often rejected, but when he gets in, he gains a huge advantage over other bidders. Personally, I would not do this, but he tells me that many debtors are surprisingly cooperative.

After doing a few of these, investors quickly become familiar with the cost of all sorts of repairs, so the estimating becomes easier and more accurate. When in doubt, talk to a contractor and check out the Bible of repair costs, "*The Home Repair and Remodel Cost Guide,*" which is published annually by Marshall and Swift.

Superior Liens

It is critical to be certain about the priority of the liens on the property before bidding. If a first-priority lien is being foreclosed, the property is being sold free and clear of other liens. If, on the other hand, a second-priority lien (like a second mortgage) is being foreclosed upon, then the property is being sold "subject to" the first priority lien. The highest bidder will buy the property with the first priority lien on it and will have to pay it off eventually. Prior to the sale, it should be announced whether the property is being sold "subject to" any other liens. Listen carefully and pay attention to details in the public notices relating to the sale to be sure that you know what you are buying

For example, in some states, liens imposed by Home Owner Associations for unpaid association dues are given "super priority," so the homeowner association liens cut ahead of the mortgage. They cannot be eliminated by a mortgage foreclosure, so in these states, if you buy a property at a mortgage foreclosure sale, you will have to pay off the home owner association liens. Of course, this added expense will have to be factored into your maximum bid.

Open (unpaid) property taxes and tax liens also have priority over mortgages, so mortgage foreclosure sales are always subject to tax liens. The winning bidder will have to pay off any open taxes on the property.

Title searches

Most investors do not obtain a title search prior to the auction because of the cost. Investors typically bid on many properties in order to win one, so they don't spend money until they have won the bid. It is critical however, to obtain title insurance immediately upon purchasing any property before you start to spend money on repairs and remodeling.

Bidding

Most sheriff's sales are open or "cry-out" auctions, where bidders call or physically signal their bids in person, in a room full of other bidders. More and more sales are being held on the Internet now, and that may be the way of the future, but as I write, bidders usually have to face off against one another, and sometimes it can get heated. I always advise newcomers to sit in on a few auctions before placing any bids. It may sound like a waste of time, but the auctions can move quickly, and a less experienced investor will learn a lot by simply watching and listening before putting any hard-earned money on the table.

Sheriff's sales are typically held at the county courthouse. Private auctions and trustee sales can be held anywhere and are usually at the property that is being sold. These sales often allow for bidders to enter and inspect the property shortly before the auction begins. This obviously reduces risks but can also increase completion of sale.

There are typically set rules for each auction, and it is critical to be familiar with them before bidding. For example, rules are strictly enforced regarding the timing and form of payment. It is quite common for a novice to forfeit a winning bid due to a misunderstanding of the payment requirements. Rules or "conditions of sale" are available prior to the auction, so be sure to be familiar with them. The conditions typically set are bidding increments, the amount of down payment, and the form of payment. Here is a sample:

MONMOUTH COUNTY SHERIFF'S OFFICE

2500 Kozloski Road
Freehold, New Jersey 07728
Phone: 732-431-6400   Fax: 732-294-5965 www.monmouthsheriff.org

---

Conditions of Sale

Please be advised that the following Conditions of Sale apply to every Sheriff's sale conducted by the Monmouth County Sheriff's Office. This is an open auction with competitive bidding. The Plaintiff will open the bidding at $1,000.00. Bidding will continue in increments of a minimum of $1,000.00 until the highest bid is reached. Upset figures *must* be disclosed by the plaintiff. By bidding at this sale you agree to and are bound by these Conditions:

1. The highest bidder, as determined by the Sheriff, shall be the purchaser. The Sheriff's decision as to the successful bidder is final. If a dispute arises as to who succeeds as the highest bidder, the Sheriff is unable to determine the successful bidder, and the dispute cannot be resolved by the Sheriff, the property will be resold.

2. The purchaser will pay twenty (20%) percent of the purchase price in cash (with a limit of $1,000), certified check or official bank check at the close of sale and sign an acknowledgment of the purchase. By participating in the sale, the purchaser agrees to be bound by the terms set forth on the acknowledgment of purchase if the purchaser is the successful bidder.

3. If the purchaser does not comply with the deposit requirements as specified above, the property will be resold.

4. All successful bidders, including the plaintiff, shall be responsible for payment of the Sheriff's fees and commissions which will be calculated on the amount of the successful bid.

5. The purchaser must pay the balance of the purchase money within thirty (30) days, which for today's sale will be _____, or the sale may be voided by the Sheriff and the property rescheduled for sale. Lawful interest will begin to accrue on the balance of the purchase price after then tenth (10) day from the date of sale. Sheriff's fees and commissions will be deducted from the bid price.

6. The sale is sold subject to unpaid taxes, assessments, water rents and such facts as an accurate survey and title search of the premises might disclose. Plaintiff shall disclose and describe the amount of such liens and encumbrances immediately prior to sale. The Sheriff is not responsible for any misrepresentations or omissions, intentional or otherwise, made by the plaintiff as to the existence and amounts of liens and encumbrances or as to the value of the asset being sold.

7. If the purchaser fails to comply with these conditions of sale, the property will be resold at a future date. The defaulting purchaser will be responsible for all such losses and expenses incurred, but receive no benefit from the second sale. Deposits will be retained by the Sheriff and disbursed by Court Order. No portion of the initial deposit monies will be credited or applied to a successive bid if made by the defaulting purchaser subsequent to a default. If the defaulting purchaser re-bids at a future sale, they will be required to submit an additional twenty (20%) percent deposit in cash (with a limit of $1,000), certified check or bank check at the close of the subsequent sale.

8. Please note that in the event of an assignment of bid, the purchaser must provide the Sheriff with the assignee's name within seven (7) days from the date of sale. Failure to provide this information will result in preparation of a deed with the original purchaser's name. If the original deed needs to be amended or replaced, a cost of $100.00 will be charged for the preparation of a new deed.

9. If the plaintiff overbids his judgement amount, plaintiff will be responsible for the surplus which will be remitted to the Court by the Sheriff for application by interested parties for turnover. The plaintiff shall also be responsible for payment of the Sheriff's fees and commissions which will be calculated on the full amount of the successful bid.

10. If a petition in bankruptcy is filed after the sale occurs, the purchaser's deposit will not be returned to the purchaser. The Sheriff will hold the deposit without interest until further directed by Court Order.

11. The recording of the Deed and any fees attached, including the realty transfer fee, is the responsibility of the purchaser.

Source: Monmouth County sheriff's website

Determining a Maximum Bid

Before you ever walk into an auction, you should have a maximum bid set, and you should never exceed your maximum bid. The maximum bid should be based on your due diligence, which led you to four estimates—estimated resale property value, estimated rehab costs, estimated carrying costs, estimated cost of paying off any priority liens and taxes—and acceptable profit (at least 20 percent of your investment):

Estimated Resale Value:	$150,000
Estimated Costs of Repairs/Rehab:	-$ 25,000
Estimated Carrying & Closing Costs:	-$ 10,000
Estimated Cost of Priority Liens:	-$ 0
Acceptable Profit:	<u>-$ 25,000</u>
Maximum Bid:	**$ 90,000**

Upset Price

Most sales result in the property being sold back to the plaintiff—the bank or creditor that filed the lawsuit leading to the sheriff's sale. This is frustrating for bidders who spend time on due diligence only to lose the bidding process. In most places, bidders can find out how high the plaintiff will bid prior to the sale. This is known as the "upset price" or "reserve price." If the plaintiff's upset price is close to, or higher than, the property value, most investors will not waste any time on it because it is very likely that the property will be sold back to the plaintiff. The bank's representative will often disclose the upset price prior to the auction because the bank pays a lower sale commission to the sheriff if no one bids. Most banks would prefer that the properties be sold to investors, but if no one is going to bid more than the upset price, the bank would prefer that no one bid at all, so the commission is not driven up. When bidding exceeds the bank's upset price, the highest bidder obtains the property, and the "surplus funds" in excess of the plaintiff bank's judgment are distributed to junior lien holders such as a second mortgage or a judgment lien holder, in order of priority.

I advise my clients to arrive early and ask the plaintiff's representative for the upset price. Mill around and listen to what the others are saying, but take it with a grain of salt. Keep in mind that the other bidders are competing with you and they may or may not be honest and forthcoming. Listen to what others are saying, but never rely upon it. A common "beginner" mistake is to bid above your predetermined maximum bid, because others were bidding more and "they must know what they are doing." Disciplined investors succeed in the long run. They stick to their plan and avoid being emotionally caught up in the competition.

Before the bidding starts, move toward the back of the room so that you can observe what is happening. Who else is bidding on your target property? Always check the rules and conditions of sale to determine the minimum bidding increment. You don't want to be guy who bids in one dollar increments. The minimum incremental bid increase is typically $100, but check to be sure. Experienced bidders who know of the plaintiff's upset price will typically start at $100 over the upset price rather than starting at $100.

Payment

Payment rules vary, but the winning bidder is typically expected to pay 5 to 20 percent at the auction in cash or bank check, and then the balance is due in a few weeks. Some jurisdictions even require payment in full on the day of the sale. If the bidder fails to make full payment, a new sale is scheduled, and the deposit can be fully or partially forfeited.

These strict payment rules make it very difficult, if not impossible, to arrange financing to bid at a sheriff's sale. A typical mortgage loan application involves a property inspection, appraisal, and financial background check. Even if preapproved, it is unlikely that a mortgage loan can be approved and closed in the short time frame between a sheriff's sale and payment deadline. Many bidders use their own savings, a home equity line of credit, personal loans from friends and family, or even credit card advances.

Bottom line: check the local rules to confirm the payment deadline and have your funds lined up before the auction. Only bid if you are sure that you want to close the deal and have the funding available.

Sheriff's or Trustee's Deed

As one would expect, delivery of the deed is often delayed. Jurisdictions vary from a few days up to a few months. The sale rules or conditions may address the timing, but the successful bidder should simply ask about the timing when paying the bid. Then, of course, follow up for the deed if it is not delivered on time. As with any other type of deed, it should be recorded immediately.

Right of Redemption

Over half of the states (including my home state, New Jersey) grant a "right of redemption" time period for the mortgage to be paid off *after* a sheriff's sale. In New Jersey, the redemption period is 10 days, but the period can be as long as 6 or even 12 months in other states. Regardless of the local state rules, if there was a federal IRS income tax lien on the property, the IRS has 120 days following a sheriff's sale to pay off. If the right of redemption is exercised, the bid payment is refunded to the investor. The investor is left disappointed having wasted time and tied up funds for no profit.

PREPARED BY:

Shaun Golden

SHERIFF'S DEED OF FORECLOSURE

Sheriff's Number:

THIS INDENTURE, made this **10th** day of **November 2015**, between Shaun Golden, Sheriff of the County of Monmouth in the State of New Jersey, party of the first part and **ivestors Inc.** party of the second part, witnesseth.

WHEREAS, on the **7th** day of **April 2015**, a certain Writ of Execution was issued out of the Superior Court of New Jersey, Chancery Division- Monmouth County, **Docket No. F0.** directed and delivered to the Sheriff of the said County of Monmouth and which said Writ is in the words or to the effect following:

THE STATE OF NEW JERSEY

TO: **THE SHERIFF OF THE COUNTY OF MONMOUTH**

GREETING:

WHEREAS, on the **7th** day of **April 2015**, by a certain judgment made in our Superior Court of New Jersey, in a certain cause therein pending, wherein the PLAINTIFF is:

: **Investors Inc.**

Attorneys for PLAINTIFFS:

Pellegrino & Feldstein, L.L.C.

and the following named parties are the DEFENDANTS:

LLC, et al

IT WAS ORDERED AND ADJUDGED that certain mortgaged premises, with the appurtenances in the Complaint, and Amendment to Complaint, if any, in the said cause particularly set forth and described: The mortgaged premises are described as set forth upon the RIDER ANNEXED HERETO AND MADE A PART HEREOF.

BEING KNOWN AS: **Tax Lot Block** of the Tax Map of **Long Branch** County of Monmouth, State of New Jersey

COMMONLY KNOWN AS: **Fourth Ave Long Branch, NJ 07740**

TOGETHER, with all and singular the rights, liberties, privileges, hereditaments and appurtenances thereunto belonging or in anywise appertaining, and the reversion and remainders, rents, issues and profits thereof, and also all the estate, right, title, interest, use, property, claim and demand of the said defendants of, in, to and out of the same, to be sold, to pay and satisfy in the first place unto the plaintiff;

Investors Inc., the sum of **$101,819.13** being the principal, interest and advances secured by a certain mortgage dated: **9/19/2007** and given by together with lawful interest thereon from **3/31/2015** until the same be paid and satisfied and also the costs of the aforesaid plaintiff with interest thereon.

The redemption period is tough on investors, because you can't rehab or resell the property until the redemption period expires. In areas with a long redemption period, investors will often pay the former owner to waive the right of redemption. Usually, the owner has no intention or ability to pay off the mortgage, or they would have paid prior to the sheriff's sale, so they are often open to this arrangement. The former owner gets some cash to waive a right that may have no value to them, and the investor eliminates the long waiting period for a low cost. This is usually accomplished through a "cash for keys" deal in which the former owner vacates the property, hands over the keys, and signs a quit claim deed and waiver of "right of redemption" in exchange for a payment. The deal often includes an extension of time before the former owner must move out.

These deals to eliminate the redemption period also prevent other investors from "stealing your deal." In jurisdictions with long redemption periods, some clever investors watch the results of sheriff's sales and then try to intervene or "raid" the deal by making a deal with the former property owner to buy the property and then exercise the right of redemption by paying off the mortgage. The former property owners are generally open to these "raiders" because (1) they have already lost the property at the sheriff's sale; (2) they have no financial ability to exercise the right of redemption by paying off the debt; and (3) they get a payment from the raider and maybe an extension of time before they must vacate the property. Of course, this only works when there is sufficient equity in the property. The property must have a higher value than the mortgage that was foreclosed and all other liens on the property. This is critical because the "raiding" investor must pay off the mortgage through the right of redemption and then pay off all other liens to clear the title.

I've used quotation marks on the terms "stealing" and "raiding" because the perception of these investors as good or bad is purely a matter of perspective. From the view of the successful bidder at the sheriff's sale, the intervening investor is a terrible person stealing a deal. The property owner, on the other hand, sees the intervening investor as a "white knight" rescuer, as discussed in Chapter 7 of this book.

I don't perceive either investor as good or bad. They are just people who are seeking profit opportunities as the rules and statutes permit. Bidders at sheriff's sales (in jurisdictions with long redemption periods) must recognize this risk, and manage the risk, by trying to make their own deals with the former owner to eliminate the redemption period.

Postsale—Now the Work Begins

Congratulations, you did some thoughtful due diligence, showed up at the sheriff's sale on time, and submitted the highest bid. You won! Now what?

The first and most critical step is to get insurance. Don't make the mistake of putting this off. It is important to manage these risks before you start to invest in rehab costs. I have had clients learn this the hard way, after spending thousands of dollars on rehab, when the property gets damaged or a title defect is discovered. Line up the following insurance coverages as soon as you win the auction:

- *Title Insurance:* Ensures that you have full and clear title that is not encumbered by any liens or claims. This is critical before you pay the full bid to the sheriff and spend any money on rehab.
- *Liability Insurance:* Insures you against any claims by third parties who may get injured on your new property.
- *Fire & Casualty Insurance:* Insures you against fire or other type of property damage.

Taking Possession

If the property is not occupied, you can change the locks and switch the utilities to your name immediately. Walk your Realtor and contractors through and make your rehab plan based on maximizing the resale price while minimizing the rehab costs.

The interior condition can be a pleasant surprise or a nightmare. I have taken possession of "dream" houses that had been cleaned out, and only needed a coat of paint, and I've walked into nightmares, where the former owner wrote nasty things on the walls and cabinets in black paint. Some people make great efforts to remove value from the house, by pulling out fixtures and even removing pipes. Although I've seen it many times, it is always disturbing.

If, on the other hand, the house is still occupied (which of course you will discover BEFORE the auction through your due diligence), then you face the delay of arranging for an eviction. The rules and procedures differ, so check with your attorney before you bid, but in most jurisdictions, you will have to arrange for a sheriff's eviction that will take weeks or even months. You can't just go and "muscle" the former owner out onto the street. In New Jersey for example, it takes a two or three months to have an eviction scheduled, and you must pay for a locksmith to change the locks and pay for a moving company to move all the furniture and personal belongings from the house into a storage facility. Oh, and you have to pay for one month of storage. Even after an eviction date has been set, the former owner can apply to a judge for a "stay of eviction."

Cash-for-Keys

Experienced investors typically try to avoid evictions by offering the former owner a monetary incentive to move out. Aside from obviously being a more compassionate approach, it can also be faster and even less expensive than the hostile eviction route.

A Word on Market Theory

So why does this work? Why does this process often result in an investor acquiring a property for less than market value? There are many reasons, but these are the three main factors:

Distressed Property: Most real estate buyers are not interested in distressed property that needs to be rehabilitated. This creates an imperfect, imbalanced market that results in below-market value sales.

Fear of the Unknown: Of the buyers who are interested in "fixer-uppers," most are scared off by unknown factors that are inherent in bidding at a foreclosure sale. As detailed above, buyers are expected to bid without inspecting the structure.

Difficult Bidding Process: Investors are required to show up at auctions where they may not be successful for weeks or months before winning the highest bid. The payment requirement also discourages most investors who don't have fast access to cash.

These factors scare away the vast majority of buyers and create a market niche that is far from "perfect." Successful sheriff's sale investors know how to manage this risk and take advantage of this very "imperfect market" by:

- Performing due diligence to gather as much information as possible—albeit incomplete;
- Making rational assumptions about the facts that cannot be discovered;
- Maintaining discipline in bidding at sales and controlling rehab costs;

Sure, everyone makes mistakes and even the most experienced investor can get burned in this area, but this is a thriving and profitable vehicle for thousands of investors.

Aside from the "unknown factor" addressed above, this market also suffers from a lack of "barrier to entry." Anyone with a line of credit can attend an auction and bid up prices. Many auctions are blown up by novices who recklessly bid up prices to heights that make it impossible to turn a fair profit. In my experience, it is harder to get a real bargain (buying at a steep discount) on low-to-mid-cost houses in nice neighborhoods. These are most attractive to novices and small investors, so the prices are often bid up too high. Novices typically shy away from the more distressed neighborhood, and higher cost auctions of over $250,000.

Tips from a Pro

Lowell Caro is a former Realtor and foreclosure specialist, and he is an administrator of the "National Foreclosure Sales Training Institute" group on LinkedIn. Lowell got started in real estate in 2002. In 2005, he started working on short sales, which led him to foreclosure sales. Lowell kindly added some of his insight:

> I always tell new investors to focus on networking to create a team of experienced professionals. There are several groups on LinkedIn.com for investors interested in foreclosure sales. I have found these online discussion groups to be a great source for networking contacts and increasing general knowledge on investing in distressed properties. You can exchange referrals, find investors, and even get free advice on specific issues.
>
> Pull together a team of people to help you with every aspect of the process. You will want a Realtor, title agent, attorney, contractors, locksmith, cleaning crew, insurance agent, landscaper, and whatever other service provider you may need. Take the time to interview your perspective teammates to ensure you like them and will be able to work well with them. Also, ensure they understand what you will be doing and are willing to go that extra mile in the event something unexpected occurs. If you are going to do multiple purchases/transactions, these service providers will want to work with you. It would be preferable to find people who have knowledge and experience specifically with what foreclosure sales entail.
>
> It may even be possible to find an experienced mentor or someone who will allow you to shadow him or her to better learn the process. If you can find an experienced investor who will help you learn, be willing to do some legwork to gain some practical experience. You want it to be a win-win for everybody involved.
>
> —Lowell Caro Jr.

Lowell has sold over 100 foreclosure properties by developing a team of people and creating a win-win situation for everyone involved. Lowell often lectures on how to invest in foreclosed properties, and he offers mentoring services.

What Can Go Wrong

Valuation Errors. The biggest risk in this investment is human error. The key is to (1) obtain an accurate valuation of the property and (2) accurately determine all liens on the property that you will have to pay off. In order to estimate property value, you have to recognize problems with the property and estimate the costs of repairs. Leaking oil tanks, wet lands, zoning issues, and structural issues will severely reduce a property value. These risks are common for all of the investment vehicles discussed in this book.

Missing Priority Liens. In many sheriff's sale auctions, the property is sold "subject to" a higher priority lien, such as a first mortgage or property-tax lien, which must be paid off by the successful bidder. Investors must be aware of these priority liens before the auction, and factor that cost into a bid.

Eviction Delays and Costs. Many properties that are sold at sheriff's sale are still occupied by the former owner, who may be difficult to evict. Eviction procedures differ, so check with your local attorney about the typical time and expenses. Factor these costs into your bid.

Rehab Delays and Costs. It is challenging to spot and then accurately budget for every necessary repair. Cost overruns are common with contractors as they run into unanticipated complications. Foreclosed houses typically have been neglected for years, so we commonly run into nightmares like leaking oil tanks, mold, frozen pipes, and even intentional damage by angry former owners. Factor in a "worst-case scenario" into your bid and add a budget line for unexpected costs.

Summary of the Pros & Cons

Pros

- ✓ **High Potential Return:** Property can often be acquired for 15 percent to 30 percent less than market value.
- ✓ **Diversity:** Investment in real estate provides a hedge against other investment asset classes such stock or bonds.
- ✓ **Control:** Investors manage risk through individual selection of notes.

- ✓ **Scalability:** There are plenty of opportunities, if your financing allows for multiple purchases.
- ✓ **Stability:** No "market swings" like the stock market or mutual funds.
- ✓ **Liquidity:** Investors can list the property for sale as soon as the deed is issued, but beware of the local "redemption period," which will delay your resale.

Cons

- ✓ **Redemption Period:** In some states, the postauction redemption period can extend for several months, delaying the process of repairing and reselling the property. This period of delay can be used by other investors to intervene and "steal" your deal.
- ✓ **Bankruptcy Delays:** Debtors may file bankruptcy to delay the eviction process.
- ✓ **Property Rehabilitation Costs:** Foreclosed properties usually require renovation and repairs before the property can be sold. These repairs can be hard to estimate, costly, and time-consuming.
- ✓ **Capital Requirements:** The cost of buying a property at sheriff's sale and repairing the property is usually over $100,000.

Hungry for More? Source Books, Consultants, Websites, and Sellers

Books

How to Buy Real Estate at Foreclosure Auctions, Marc Sherby
Foreclosure Investing for Dummies, Ralph R. Roberts
Idiot's Guide to Buying Foreclosures, Dempsey & Beitler
The Home Repair and Remodel Cost Guide, Marshall and Swift.

Websites

Check your local sheriff's department sites
LinkedIn.com
Zillow.com
Trulia.com
Redfin.com
PropertyShark.com
RapidTrusteeSale.com

7

"White Knight" Rescues & Short Sales

Buying Preforeclosure Property

Here is a chance to be the "Good Guy." Most of the other investments discussed in this book involve acquiring and collecting debt from people who are unable to pay. This one is different, but it isn't easy.

In the previous two chapters we've addressed buying properties at sheriff's sales, and buying notes to foreclose upon. This chapter is closely related, but we are coming from a different angle. Investors identify pending foreclosures where the owner has equity, meaning the property is worth more than the amount that is owed on the foreclosure. The investor then "rescues" the owner by buying the property from the owner before the foreclosure is completed. It is a rare "win-win" solution—the investor acquires the distressed property at a below-market price, the bank gets paid off, and the owner avoids being foreclosed upon, walking away with a portion of the equity that he or she had built up in the property. The challenge is sifting through many foreclosures and finding the "perfect storm" scenario where the owner (1) has equity; (2) has not taken the necessary steps to unlock the equity; and (3) is willing to deal with you before the pending foreclosure ends.

This investment is not directly buying debt, but it derives from the debt collection process. Investors acquire distressed property at a discount due to an impending debt collection action. The debtor who is about to lose his property (along with any equity) perceives preforeclosure buyers as "good guys" or "white knights." On the other hand, the bank or investor that is foreclosing and the sheriff's sale bidder may see preforeclosure buyers as "bad guys" who raid their deals and steal their profits.

The risks are relatively low. There is no holding period or long foreclosure process during which the property may change value. This opportunity involves a simple purchase of property "as is," after the property is fully inspected, so you know what you are getting and you get the keys at closing. The challenge is finding these opportunities.

Summary Points

1. **Specialized Knowledge:** Property values, searching public records
2. **Minimum Capital Requirement:** Greatly varies from $50,000 and up
3. **Scalability:** Yes; many potential opportunities but requires a lot of time and effort
4. **Liquidity:** Yes, real estate is easy to sell if the resale market is strong
5. **Priority over Other Forms of Debt:** Low. Property is purchased subject to all liens.
6. **Barriers to Entry:** Cash required and time-consuming

Find Pending Foreclosures in Your Area

Investors have to do a lot of homework. The investor must sift through lists of active foreclosures. This information is public record, but the access varies by state. Many websites offer foreclosure lists for a price, but the data are often stale. Your results will vary depending on your region, but here are a few sources:

✓ County records of Lis Pendens filings, which reveal foreclosures. Investors may search for recorded Lis Pendens themselves or pay a title search company to provide lists.
✓ Court webpages often provide limited access to public filings such as foreclosure complaints.
✓ Sheriff's department webpages often list upcoming sales.

- ✓ Public notices in newspapers.
- ✓ Foreclosure lists from Zillow.com and other real estate Internet sites.
- ✓ Short sale listing in Realtors' multiple listing service ("MLS") websites.
- ✓ Running ads in craigslist.com and newspapers offering to help debtors who are unable to pay their mortgage.
- ✓ Word of mouth including local attorneys and Realtors who may be aware of distressed debtors

The most common approach is simply to search through real estate listings in the online multiple listing sites. Short sales are identified right in the listings.

Testing for Equity

The vast majority of foreclosures are underwater, meaning the lien or liens are greater than the property value, so there is no room for a standard "White Knight" rescue. The goal here is to screen for owners who have equity—the home value is higher than all liens on the property. Again, you will have to become fairly acquainted with the public records in your area. The foreclosure details that you have found will usually provide the payoff value of the lien that is being foreclosed.

Then you must determine the "as is" current value of the property. Most investors work with a local Realtor who can easily provide a Broker's Price Opinion ("BPO") for the property value. If you don't work with a Realtor, you can compare recent sales data from online Multiple Listing Services to generate your own valuation.

Once you compare the loan payoff value to the property value, you can make an *initial* screening for equity.

Property Value As Is:	$250,000
Payoff Value of Lien in Foreclosure:	-$150,000
Equity Potential:	$100,000

This example indicates *potential* equity of $100,000 so it would pass the initial screening of just the property value and the payoff value of the pending foreclosure. You are only halfway there, however, because you must factor in any other liens on the property such as second mortgages, property tax liens, condo liens, money judgment liens, and IRS tax liens.

Liens are recorded and are public record, so once you have found a property that passes the initial screening, you must do a public record search to determine any other liens on the property. You will be buying this property "subject to" all liens, so you will have to pay them all off at some point.

Property Value As Is:	$250,000
Payoff Value of Lien in Foreclosure:	-$150,000
Property Tax Liens:	-$ 10,000
Money Judgment Liens:	-$ 30,000
IRS Tax Lien:	-$ 60,000
Equity:	$ 0

In this example, you can see how there can be no equity, even when the property passes the initial screening. Investors must be detailed and thorough to avoid costly mistakes.

Here is an example that would be attractive:

Property Value As Is:	$250,000
Payoff Value of Lien in Foreclosure:	-$100,000
Property Tax Liens:	-$ 10,000
Money Judgment Liens:	-$ 20,000
IRS Tax Lien:	-$ 20,000
Equity:	$ 100,000

Short Sales

If there is no equity, it is much more difficult to make a "rescue" deal. It would require one or more of the lien holders to agree to accept less than the amount due on their lien. This is often called a "short payment." It is much harder to organize a deal like this, but it is possible. Why would a lien holder agree to take less than the amount of their lien? It is always better to get something than to get nothing. The pending foreclosure would eliminate all junior (lower priority) liens, so junior lien holders have incentive to see a deal work—even if they get paid much less than the amount of their lien.

While it is harder to put together a "short sale rescue," it is worth consideration because there are many more of these opportunities available.

Property Value As Is:	$250,000	
	Lien Value	Short Payment
Payoff Value of Lien in Foreclosure:	-$150,000	-$150,000 (Fully Paid)
Property Tax Liens:	-$ 10,000	-$ 10,000 (Fully Paid)
Money Judgment Liens:	-$ 30,000	-$ 10,000 (Short Pay)
IRS Tax Lien:	-$ 60,000	-$ 60,000 (Fully Paid)
Equity:	$ 0	$ 20,000

This example illustrates how a deal can be made to create $20,000 in free equity if the lowest priority judgment lien holder could be persuaded to accept $10,000 (instead of $30,000). The judgment lien would be eliminated if the foreclosure were to be completed, so the judgment holder would be wise to agree to a short payment of $10,000. Note that the highest-priority tax lien holder would not agree to any reduction because of the high priority.

Tips From a Pro

Art Matuschat is a Realtor in New Jersey who specializes in short sales. Through his company, New Jersey Realty Solutions, Art publishes a newsletter on short sales and puts dealmakers together with deals. Because he has been finding and working out short sales for over fifteen years, I asked Art to contribute some of his experience in this chapter.

There are some great deals that you can find right at your fingertips. Yes, I am talking about the Multiple Listing Service ("MLS"). which anyone can search on the Internet. Of course, the once-in-a-lifetime "blockbuster" deals are more commonly found in places other than the MLS, but they are rare and hard to find, so don't forget to search the MLS. Approximately 80 percent of all home sales are sold through Realtors on the MLS. It is estimated that 10 percent of the MLS listings are good deals for investors. According to Homes.com, as of August 2016 in just New Jersey, there are approximately 100,000 homes for sale, so there are about 10,000 opportunities for an attractive investment on the MLS.
—Art Matuschat, NewJerseyRealtySolutions.com

Making Contact

Once you have done your research and crunched the numbers to find viable candidates, it can be very difficult and time-consuming to get through to the debtor. They are scared, skeptical, and behind a closed door. They typically have several creditors calling and writing repeated letters threatening lawsuits. They are usually embarrassed and don't want to talk about it. It takes persistence and patience to get through to them, but it is possible, and I know investors who make a living doing just this.

There is no "best" way to make contact. Most investors send letters, and some also call or make personal visits, leaving notes on the door when the owner won't answer.

The people who you are trying to reach are all different. They have different personalities and varying sensitivities. The approach that works for some may alienate others. It is usually helpful if you are introduced by a mutual friend.

Investors who succeed in this area have a persistent, professional, and polite approach. They have strong people skills and can listen with empathy. Most important, they cast a wide net because it is a numbers game. They mail a letter or postcard to every foreclosure property in their target area and then try to screen those who respond for a potential deal. The more debtors that you try to reach, the more debtors you will reach. An investor whom I interviewed as part of my research for this book told me that he has a hit ratio of about 2 to 3 percent. He must identify and attempt to contact 100 potential "rescues" in order to make just two or three deals.

Making a Deal

This is another time to be creative. Be open and honest with the debtor and gain an understanding of his or her concerns and priorities. If the debtor's main priority is extending possession of their home, then consider a deed and lease back. Perhaps they can afford to pay a fair rent but just can't pay off the lien that is being foreclosed. That scenario is common and could create an attractive investment return.

On the other hand, if the debtor has accepted the idea of vacating the home, the focus can be on cash to get resettled elsewhere. Just structure an offer that maximizes a cash buyout.

Investors must also have the discipline to walk away from a deal that isn't adding up even after having spent a few days crunching numbers and talking to the owner and creditors. You can't save everyone. If the numbers don't add up, just explain it to the owner and walk away.

Why This Works

There are two scenarios covered in this chapter—properties that are being foreclosed upon **with equity** or **without equity ("short sales")**. Each scenario has a different set of forces that create this opportunity.

Preforeclosures <u>With</u> Equity

When I talk to people about this opportunity, they always ask the same question: "If the owner has equity in the property and can't afford to stop the foreclosure by paying off the lien, then why doesn't the owner refinance, file bankruptcy, or just sell on the open market through a Realtor?" It is a fair question. If all debtors were unemotional, made rational decisions, and had a basic understanding of their options, this investment vehicle would not exist. There would also be a lot fewer foreclosures. Unfortunately, there are many foreclosure debtors who simply cannot deal with their situation. Some are too emotionally distraught. Others are simply overwhelmed and put their head in the sand, rather than deal with the issue.

Over the past twenty years as a foreclosure attorney, I have spoken with hundreds of people who have lost their home to foreclosure, and many have told me that when they received the foreclosure notices, they knew they lacked funds to pay, so they just prayed and "left it in God's hands." These debtors have valuable equity in their property and just need guidance to unlock the equity before the foreclosure is completed. There is free assistance available, such as free legal consultation, government social services, and Realtors, but many people won't seek help or, worse yet, don't even know how to ask. Many tell themselves, "I'll deal with it tomorrow," but they never do. This inability to take action creates the opportunity for investors to make money by helping the debtor keep some of their equity.

Preforeclosures <u>Without</u> Equity ("Short Sales")

Short sale opportunities are driven by the banks simply being inundated with more properties than they can manage. Most banks would rather cash out for less money early, rather than do the undertaking hard work to squeeze out extra dollars at a later date. Many banks also lack the *local* knowledge and experience that is needed to quickly and efficiently turn around a distressed property.

This may seem counterintuitive, but the **best** deals are usually made on the **worst**-looking properties. It is hard to get the seller or bank to accept a bargain price on a house that is in great shape because there is always a line of potential buyers for "cream puff" houses. It is much easier to get a great price on a property that is in bad shape. I look for houses that look like no one in their right mind would ever buy them. If a typical "retail" buyer wouldn't even step foot through the door, then you can make a nice deal.

As detailed above, it is far from easy to reach the owners and make a deal with them, so there is very limited competition among investors in this market. This difficulty creates the niche that allows for attractive deals for investors who have the ability.

Tips From a Pro

I like homes in disrepair because I can exhaustively enumerate the flaws to the bank in order to get a discounted value on the home. Homes with a laundry list of repairs spell loss and risk to the bank and cause the bankers to discount the property. If you do your homework right, any house can be renovated and resold for a nice profit.

On the other hand, homes that are in good shape will typically attract a crowd of "retail" buyers who drive up the price. As Mike has discussed throughout this book, it is the inefficiency or imperfection of a market that creates larger profits.

—Art Matuschat, NewJerseyRealtySolutions.com

What Can Go Wrong

Valuation Errors. The biggest risk in this investment is human error. The key is to (1) obtain an accurate valuation of the property and (2) accurately determine all liens on the property that you will have to pay off. In order to estimate property value, you have to recognize problems with the property and estimate the costs of repairs. Leaking oil tanks, wet lands, zoning issues, and structural issues will severely reduce a property value. These risks are common for all of the investment vehicles discussed in this book.

Value of Your Time. Be prepared for rejection and a high failure rate. In fact, you will find that your efforts and insights often "wake up" or educate the owner, and they take other action to preserve their equity such as filing bankruptcy or selling to someone else. No one likes to invest time without out being rewarded, but take some satisfaction in having helped someone who needed it.

An investor must consider the time that it takes to find these deals. Your time is worth money. Experienced investors weigh how their time and money could be put to use elsewhere—"opportunity cost." If your time, experience, and money can be used more profitably in other endeavors, then move on.

Regulatory Limits. Many states have rules that limit or prohibit practices known as "title raiding" or "heir hunting." For example, in New Jersey, there is a law that imposes strict limitations an investors who try to buy property while that property is the subject of a tax lien foreclosure. It is well beyond the scope of this book to address every possible legal limitation is every state, so be sure to consult with an experienced local attorney.

Summary of the Pros & Cons

Pros

- ✓ **Low Risk:** Investors fully inspect the property and review a title search prior to purchasing, so, unlike most investments discussed in this book, there are no unknown variables.
- ✓ **Diversity:** Investment in real estate provides a hedge against other investment asset classes such as stock or bonds.
- ✓ **Control:** Investors have full knowledge and control over the negotiation, rehab, and resale process.
- ✓ **Helping Others**: Preforeclosure rescue deals help a debtor from losing equity that the owner accumulated in the subject property. Investors help a debtor who is in need of rescue.
- ✓ **Stability:** No "market swings" like the stock market or mutual funds.

Cons

- ✓ **Time-consuming:** Viable deals are difficult to find and negotiate.

Hungry for More? Source Books, Consultants, Websites, and Sellers

Books

Idiot's Guide to Buying Foreclosures, Dempsey & Beitler

8

REO & Seized Assets
Buying Foreclosed Property from Banks

This chapter is more straightforward and simple than most of the others. Property that has been foreclosed upon and taken by a bank is known as "REO" ("real estate owned"). Buying REO property is the same as buying any other piece of real estate, except the seller is more motivated with no emotional attachment to the property, and the property is sold "as is" typically in run-down condition. REO properties are normally listed with real estate brokers in the Multiple Listing Service, and the seller is typically a bank or other financial company with hundreds of distressed properties to unload. Unlike most of the other investments discussed in this book, the investor has a full opportunity to inspect the property and obtain mortgage financing like any other real estate purchase.

The challenge is entirely based on accurately assessing the property condition and efficiently making repairs.

Like Chapter 7 on buying preforeclosures, this investment is not directly buying debt, but it derives from the debt collection process. Investors acquire property at a discount due to its distressed condition created by a debt collection action.

The risks are relatively low. There is no holding period or long foreclosure process during which the property may change value. This opportunity involves a simple purchase of property "as is," after the property is fully inspected, so you know what you are getting and you get the keys at closing. The opportunities are plentiful and advertised by Realtors. It is all about managing the rehab. Unfortunately, because risks are low, the chance of large profits is also low. Low risk, low return.

Too Close to "Perfect Market"

As detailed in the introductory portion of this book, it is very difficult to achieve unusually large profits in a market that is too close to "perfect." Buying foreclosed REO property from banks has many characteristics of a perfect market:

- ✓ Open Competition: Publicly advertised through brokers and Multiple Listing Services.
- ✓ Information: Buyers may fully inspect properties before bidding.
- ✓ No Restrictions: No licensing or financial barriers to restrict competition.
- ✓ Specialized Knowledge: No specialized knowledge or training required.
- ✓ Easy Financing: Buyers may use standard mortgage financing.

Finding REO Properties to Buy

REO is typically thought of as "bank"-owned, but a variety of creditors foreclose upon and sell properties including credit unions, insurance companies, hedge funds, private individuals, and government agencies such as FNMA and HUD. The vast majority of REOs are listed in and sold through Realtors' multiple listing services. REOs can also be found listed in:

- Bank websites
- Government agency websites, like HUD, FNMA
- Public auction noticed published in newspapers and online

Making an Offer

If an REO property is listed by a Realtor (as most are), offers must be submitted in writing through the listing Realtor. The only practical difference is that since the seller is a bank, financial institution, or government agency, it can take several weeks or even months to receive a response. This is because there usually are several layers of review before your offer is approved or accepted. The waiting period can be frustrating, so be prepared for it. Use that time to evaluate other properties for your next target.

Another key difference is that all offers for REOs should be accompanied by a written preapproval letter from your lender to establish that you will qualify for the mortgage that you need to buy the property. If you intend to buy the property without financing it is even better, but your offer should include a written proof of funds, such as a copy of your bank account revealing sufficient funds to close.

Certain REO properties are listed for sale with a legal restriction that they cannot be sold for less than the asking price. If the listing includes a line like *property to be sold as is only and is subject to HUD Guidelines 24 CFR 206.125,"* it means that the property was acquired through foreclosure of a reverse mortgage and the seller will not consider reduced offers. This is a federal regulation and they are serious, so don't waste a lot of time unless you are prepared to pay full asking price. There are circumstances under which the seller can eventually lower the price, but in my experience, offers under the listing price will not be accepted.

As is

REO properties are also listed and sold "as is" meaning the seller will not make any repairs. Your offer must reflect the "as is" condition of the property. Use the Due Diligence Checklist at the end of this book to assist in assessing repairs.

Occupied?

Some REO property is sold with the former owner or a tenant still occupying the property. There is a good and bad side to this. The good side is that an investor can typically get a much better price for taking the property occupied. The bad side is that you will have to deal with the eviction. See Chapter 6 for a discussion on how best to take possession.

Valuation

The biggest challenge is in determining the value of the property. The task is much easier for buying REOs than it is for buying at a sheriff's sale because investors have full and repeated access into the property and may rely on help from Realtors, licensed home inspectors, and contractors to find all of the flaws and determine the costs of repair. See Chapter 6 on sheriff's sales for a detailed discussion on how to determine the "as is" value of a property.

The ultimate goal is to determine how much you are willing to pay for the property in its current condition. The best way to do that is to "back into it" by determining what you could sell it for after it is fixed up for resale, and then subtracting how much it would cost you to get the property into that resale condition. In order to calculate the maximum bid, an investor must estimate three values:

- What will the property be worth after it is fixed up and resold? To do this, we look at what prices for which similar properties have recently sold.
- What will be the cost of the repairs?
- What will the carrying and resale costs be? This includes your cost of funds (interest), insurance, property taxes, utilities, condo fees (if applicable), recording fees, inspection fees, attorney fees, and Realtor commissions.

Why it Works:

Why can an investor acquire REO for less than its actual market value? In short: over-supply. Banks and financial companies that acquire REOs through foreclosure are less inclined to hold out for the best possible offer. The officers are charged with the job of clearing the books, so they are motivated to sell quickly, even when a quick sale requires accepting a low offer. As noted at the beginning of this chapter, this is not the place to look for "home run deals." The listing Realtors earn their commission and retain their clients by getting fair prices for these properties. The MLS system is well designed to generate demand, so it is rare to find a "steal."

What Can Go Wrong

Valuation Errors. The biggest risk in this investment is human error in assessing the current condition and calculating the ultimate value of the property. In order to estimate property value, you have to recognize problems with the property and estimate the costs of repairs. Leaking oil tanks, wet lands, zoning issues, and structural issues will severely reduce a property value. ***Use the Property Due Diligence Checklists included at the end of this book.*** These risks are common for all of the investment vehicles discussed in this book.

Summary of the Pros & Cons

Pros

- ✓ **Low Risk:** Investors fully inspect the property and review a title search prior to purchasing, so unlike most investments discussed in this book, there are no unknown variables.
- ✓ **Diversity:** Investment in real estate provides a hedge against other investment asset classes such as stock or bonds.
- ✓ **Control:** Investors have full knowledge and control over the negotiation, rehab, and resale process.
- ✓ **Stability:** No "market swings" like the stock market or mutual funds.

Cons

- ✓ **Low Reward:** Outsized, market-beating profits are difficult to achieve due to the efficiency of the MLS real estate market.

Hungry for More? Source Books, Consultants, Websites, and Sellers

Books

Idiot's Guide to Buying Foreclosures, Bobbi Dempsey & Todd Beitler

9

Life Settlements and Viaticals
Buying Life Insurance Benefits

Most investors haven't heard of life settlements, and those who are aware of this opportunity usually do not have a full and fair understanding of the pros and cons. It is relatively easy, with no specialized knowledge or experience required, but there are a few unattractive aspects. The process is simple. An agent will arrange the deal for you and get you all of the information and documents that you need. Best of all, the debt is paid by a regulated "A"-rated insurance company, which is about as secure as you can get.

Investors buy a life insurance policy from a "life settlement" company that buys life insurance policies from people who do not want the life insurance policy any longer. The insured person is selling the policy because he or she wants to "cash out" for a price that is higher than the "cash value" that the life insurance company would pay, and less than the full death benefit that will be paid out upon settlement of the life insurance policy.

The policy holder must be at least 65 years of age, and the insurance policy must be aged beyond the time for any challenge by the insurance company, so the investor acquires a contractual right to be paid by an "A"-rated life insurance company upon the death of the insured. Investors buy the policies at attractive discounts to the eventual payoff value, so the profit is determined and locked in when the investment is made. Everyone has heard the old saying about "buying low and selling high." Here is an opportunity to buy a rock-solid future payment for a deep discount. No research, no economic predictions, no market fluctuations. The only questions is when will the policy pay off, and can you trust the life settlement company that structures the transaction?

Why Would a Policy Holder Sell a Life Insurance Policy?

People buy life insurance for many reasons, and over the course of their life, circumstances change, making the policy unnecessary. Many people buy a life insurance policy when they land their first job or get married. Years later, if they are widowed with no children or close heirs, they have no reason to maintain the policy. Others simply can't afford the annual premiums or need cash. Many people retire with what seems

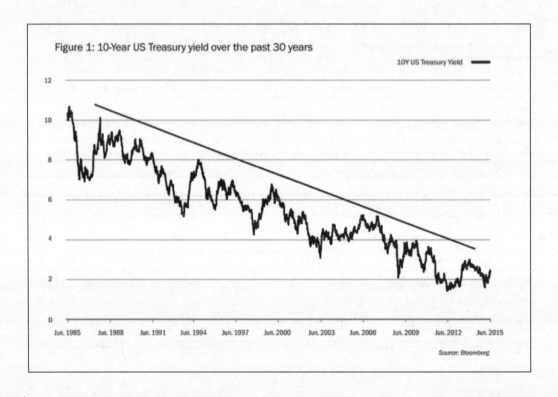

Figure 1: 10-Year US Treasury yield over the past 30 years

Source: Bloomberg

to be sufficient savings and a well-planned budget, only to see their financial stability destroyed by the volatility of the stock market and artificially depressed interest rates. Anyone who retired a few years ago planning to earn interest of 4–5 percent on bank savings was in for a nasty surprise as bank interest rates have plummeted to under 1 percent. The chart above illustrates how treasury bond yields have plummeted in recent years, leaving fixed-income investors in a financial squeeze.

Current interest rates make it very difficult to survive on most retirement budgets. Many retirees are faced with tough financial decisions, and they find the idea of selling a life insurance policy to be more appealing than alternatives such as selling their home.

Some common reasons for a policy holder to sell a life insurance policy include:

- No longer can afford annual premium payments on the policy;
- No longer has a need for the policy due to changed circumstances such as no heirs;
- Need for immediate cash payment for medical, housing, or other pressing needs;
- Federal estate tax laws have changed, increasing the exemption limits, so many life insurance policies that were purchased for estate planning have become less important.

Too Morbid for You?

If you are sensing an "ick" factor as you read this, you are not alone. Most investors feel at least hesitant about profiting on someone's death. It is certainly understandable if you feel that this investment option is not for you. In fact, I have not personally invested in this field. Before you turn to the next chapter, however, just consider a few factors:

1. **Helping the Insured.** As addressed above, there are several rational and compelling reasons for some policy holders to sell their policies. As more investors learn about and accept this opportunity, the increased demand will lead to higher sale values for the people who decide to sell. If the insured defaults on premium payments, the policy is cancelled, and the insured gets nothing. If the insured returns the policy to the insurance company for its cash value, he or she will receive less than the sale value. There is no question that policy holders who choose to "cash out" get a benefit from selling.

2. **No Moral Difference from an Inheritance**. Most of us have inherited, or will inherit, money through an estate or life insurance policy at some point

in our lives. I have never heard of anyone turning down an inheritance or life insurance payment because they don't want to "profit on the death" of another. Why should this investment vehicle be different? In fact, the investor provides financial assistance to the insured, so it could be argued that the investor is on higher moral ground than an heir who, in most cases, provides no financial assistance to the policy holder.

3. **Dealing with an Agent and Insurance Company.** Investors have nothing to do with the policy holder who has already made the decision to sell the life insurance policy. The investor deals entirely with (1) a life settlement agency that brokers the sale and (2) a life insurance company that is already obligated to make payment whether the policy is sold or not.

4. **Significant Investment and Risk**. Aside from the purchase price, investors may have to make annual premium payments for an undetermined period of years before receiving payment. Investors take risk and pay for the reward. There is no windfall or undeserved gain.

Risks?

Aside from the "ick factor" discussed above, there are a few risks that must be carefully managed:

1. **Extension Risk.** There is no way to be sure when the investment will pay off, because there is no way to predict when the insured will pass away. Investors are guaranteed a certain payoff, but as the term is extended, the return on investment is decreased. This is the main risk, and investors manage this risk by spreading their investments among several different deals (as discussed in detail below).

2. **Credit Risk.** Stability of the insurance company is critical, but easily managed. This is a very low risk because life insurance companies are heavily regulated. Most investors will only invest in a life settlement where the policy is issued by an "A"-rated life insurance company that is licensed and regulated in the US No fly-by-night insurance companies based in a foreign island beyond the reach of US regulators.

3. **Interest Rate Risk.** As with any investment in debt, timing of repayment is important because market conditions change. As interest rates increase, new investments yield higher returns, so older investments generally become less desirable. Will you miss out on higher interest rates while you are waiting for the life insurance policy to be paid off?

4. **Fraud.** This is the risk that is hardest to manage, and which drives many would-be investors away. There have been many reported scams and Ponzi schemes orchestrated by fraudulent life settlement companies. The typical scenario is for the life settlement company to sell shares in life insurance policies that do not really exist. The life settlement companies are not large, well-known firms, so it is very difficult to reach a level of comfort with them. This is my personal reason why I have not invested in life settlements.

Credit Risk?

One of the attractive aspects of investing in life settlements is the low credit risk, which is the risk of a debt not being repaid. Most of the other chapters in this book include large sections addressing how the debt can be collected through lawsuits, foreclosures, sheriff's sales, evictions, etc. Investors who buy life settlements face extremely low credit risk because the debt is owed by life insurance companies that are considered to be about as financially stable as any private company can be.

Life insurance companies are regulated by each state and are required to maintain reserves to cover all liabilities. They are inspected by state regulators, and if reserves fall too low, they are placed into receivership and sold to larger life insurance companies. Several life insurance companies have existed for over a hundred years through the World Wars, the Great Depression, the dot com stock market crash, etc. Warren Buffet's "Berkshire Hathaway" company invests in life insurance companies, and the largest US banks hold billions of dollars in life insurance policies. Nothing is absolutely certain in life, but "A"-rated domestic life insurance companies are about as close as you will see. Of course, investors should stick with policies issued by "A"-rated life insurance companies with recognizable brand names and licensed in the US—nothing based in some tropical island.

How Is This Done?

There are several life settlement companies that advertise to find sellers and package the investment for buyers. The life settlement agent will collect information about the life insurance policy and the policy holder so investors can evaluate the deal. The key factors include:

- Age of the (seller) policy holder
- Medical records of the policy holder
- Lifestyle of the policyholder

- Life insurance policy
- Life expectancy report from an independent actuarial company that provides a written assessment of the insured's life expectancy based on death rates for people with similar age, medical records, and lifestyles.

The life settlement company then presents the data to potential investors, who decide whether to buy the policy and how much to offer. The life settlement company typically receives a fee upon closing the sale and then another fee when the policy pays off.

Life Settlement vs Viaticals

Life settlement is the term for the sale of any life insurance policy. States regulate the transactions, so the rules and limitations vary a bit state by state. States generally impose the following rules:

- The "insured" (person who is selling the insurance policy) must be over 62;
- The insurance policy must be matured—typically at least two years since the creation of the policy;
- The insured must sign a medical record release so an accurate health and actuarial assessment can be prepared;
- A neutral third party must provide an actuarial report to estimate the average life expectancy for a typical person with similar health and lifestyle attributes of the insured.

A *viatical* is a type of life settlement where the insured is terminally ill with a limited life expectancy of two years or less. Viaticals are priced higher—closer to the amount of the death benefit due to the relatively short expected payment term, but advances in medical treatments may extend the payment term.

Viaticals gained popularity in the 1980s due to the HIV epidemic. Effective treatments had not been established, and many young people sought to cash out of their life insurance policies.

Managing against Extension Risk

The main risk is that the insured will outlive the expected life term, thereby delaying the investor's payoff—*Extension Risk*. This risk hurts investors in two ways:

1. Delayed payment reduces the investor's annualized return on investment. If a $100 investment generates a $50 profit in one year, it is a 50 percent annual

profit. If it takes two years, it is a 25 percent annualized return, and if it drags on for 10 years, then the annualized return is reduced to just 5 percent. The investor still generates a $50 profit on a $100 investment, but the timing changes the results drastically.

2. Premium payments also eat into profits. Some life insurance policies are sold with premiums that have been "paid up," so the investor will not have to make any annual premium payments to maintain the policy. Most policies, however, are not "paid up," so the investor must be prepared to pay the annual premium each year until the policy pays off. This obviously cuts into profits and must be priced into the deal.

Some life settlement companies arrange for insurance to address the risk of the investment not maturing in the time expected. For an additional cost, of course, an insurance bond can be obtained to pay the investor if the life settlement does not conclude in the time frame anticipated in the life expectancy report. Of course, the terms vary based on each insurance bond, but typically the investor will receive his investment back along with a market rate interest if the life settlement does not pay off by a set date. This is an interesting option, as it manages the main risk, but it can be costly. Also, the insurance bond is purchased by the life settlement agent, so there is an added risk that the agent may default on its obligation to obtain the bond and to pay the proceeds to the investors. Investors should insist on getting a copy of the insurance bond and only deal with reputable life settlement companies. A list of the larger life settlement companies is included below.

Fractioning

Another way to address extension risk is through "fractioning," where a life insurance policy is sold to a group of investors rather than to a single investor. This allows for greater diversification by spreading an investor's funds among many life settlements rather than just one or two. Similar to investing in a mutual fund of stocks rather than a single stock, the investor spreads risk, so the investment is more likely to perform as expected. By investing in many smaller deals, each investor is more likely to experience a more even and anticipated result because the outlying, unexpected results from quick payoffs and slow payoffs are spread out and shared among many investors.

Another advantage is that the annual premiums are shared among the pool of investors. Some life settlement agents will arrange for the investors to escrow sufficient funds to pay the annual premium payments for the anticipated term of the deal, so that the investors will not have to contribute any further funds as long as the life settlement deal matures as expected. If the payoff is extended beyond the term anticipated, then the investors will have to contribute more funds each year to pay the premium. What happens if one or more of the investors fails to contribute his or her share of the annual premium? Be sure that if you invest in a fractioned or "pooled" deal, this contingency is addressed in writing.

Of course, "fractioning" or "pooling" adds some expense for the trustee's fees, and it minimizes the chance of favorable outlying results from quick payouts. Fractioning also adds a level of risk in the trust that holds the policy for the investors. In a typical life settlement, the life insurance policy is assigned directly to the investor. In fractioned arrangements, the policy is held in trust for all of the investors, so investors must be comfortable with the trustee. I find this risk hard to get past because the trustees are typically small, local companies run by an attorney or former insurance agent. I've watched too many episodes of "American Greed" to trust the "trustee" unless the trustee is a federal agency or a large "household name" bank or insurance company.

Qualified Investors Only

Unfortunately, there are also some net worth and income requirements. In most states, investors must have either a net worth of at least one million US dollars, excluding the value of one's primary residence, or have income of at least $200,000 each year for the last two years (or $300,000 combined income if married).

Pricing

Pricing is not set in stone and depends on the demand from investors. This is one of the challenges that investors face, because there is no public listing of prices like the stock exchanges. Generally, the price that an investor pays to buy a life settlement is based on these factors:

1. Amount of the death benefit that will be paid upon the death of the insured;
2. Amount of the annual premiums that the investor will have to pay until the policy is paid in full or until the insured passes away;
3. Life expectancy for the insured.

For example, if you could buy a $75,000 life insurance policy for $20,000, and there was an additional $15,000 to be paid in premiums, plus $2,500 in commissions, the investment analysis would be as follows:

$75,000	Insurance Death Benefit payment from Insurance Co. to Investor
-$20,000	Initial Investment Paid to Buy the Life Insurance Policy
-$15,000	Remaining Annual Premium Payments to be Made by Investor
-$ 2,500	Commission
$37,500	TOTAL PROJECTED PROFIT

This projected $37,500 profit would be quite attractive on an investment of $20,000, but the issue (like many things in life) is timing. If the policy paid off in just two years, then you'd have doubled your investment in two years for an annualized return of 50 percent. That would clearly be an unusual outcome—a home run. If, however, the insured has a nice long life of another twenty years, your near $38,000 profit would equate to an annualized return of just 5 percent.

$1.65 Billion Market

In 2016, *The Deal*, a financial media firm, issued results from its annual survey of the life settlement market, revealing that life settlement transactions increased 32.6 percent in 2015. Despite the large increase in deals, the face value of the policies was about the same as the previous year, $1.65 billion. This survey confirms that the life settlement market is large and strong, with more deals involving smaller policies.

According to the survey, 1,123 life insurance policies were sold for a total of $325 million. The top five life settlement buyers in 2015:

Life Settlement Co.	# of Policies Purchased	Face Value of Policies	Amount paid
1. **Life Equity LLC**	181	$332.78 million	$31.42 million
2. **Coventry First LLC**	168	$108.78 million	$22.91 million
3. **Abacus Settlements LLC**	106	$184.53 million	$53.81 million
4. **GWG Life LLC**	105	$180.37 million	$38.04 million
5. **Settlement Group Inc.**	93 settlements	$ 87.43 million	$ 7.6 million

What About The Sellers?

This is an investment book, so of course we are focused on the buyer's side of the transaction, but it always helps to understand the other side of a transaction. The amount that a seller will receive from selling a policy will always be greater than the cash surrender value and less than the death benefit value. This chart published by the *Life Insurance Settlement Association* illustrates the comparison between surrendering a life insurance policy for its cash value compared to selling the policy or holding it to maturity:

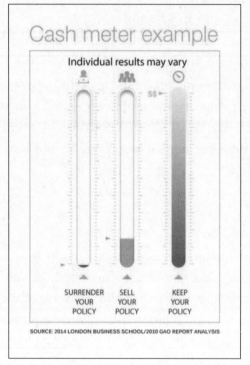

Of course, holding the policy for the eventual death benefit provides the highest payoff, but people who sell their policy have pressing reasons to cash out. Independent studies of life settlement deals have confirmed that sellers receive at least four times more than the cash value of the policy.

> "Americans who sold their unwanted life insurance policies collectively received more than four times the amount they would have received had they surrendered them to their life insurance companies."
>
> —London Business School Study, 2014

> "US policy owners received 4-8 times more than the policy cash surrender values from life settlements from 2006-2009."
> —US Government Accountability Office (GAO) Study, 2010

We have already addressed a few of the reasons why an insured may want (or need) to sell a life insurance policy, but here is a basic summary of the issues that sellers must face:

- *Pricing.* There is no organized market with publicly listed pricing, so it is difficult for sellers to determine whether they are getting a fair price for their life insurance policy unless they shop around, offering the policy to several agents. Generally, a seller should expect to get about four to five times the cash value of the policy.
- *Fees.* Fees and commissions are often high. Both buyers and sellers should ask for a list of all fees and commissions.
- *Cash Value.* Whole life policies have a "cash value" that the insurance company would pay to cancel the policy. Sellers should obtain the current cash value and expect to receive a net sale price of about four to five times the cash value.
- *Tax & Public Assistance.* A large payment from the sale of a policy could trigger negative implications if the seller received benefits such as food stamps, Medicaid, or social security. A portion of the sale proceeds maybe taxable.
- *Medical Records.* In order to sell a life insurance policy, the insured must be willing to disclose current medical conditions and medical records to the agent and buyer. The buyer may periodically make future medical health inquiries, so be aware of the process and limitations of these periodic health inquiries.
- *Buyer's Identity.* The seller must be aware that an investor will have a financial interest in the seller's death.
- *New Insurance?* Sellers often intend to use a portion of the sale proceeds to buy a smaller or less costly policy. In this scenario, the seller should confirm the cost of the new policy before selling the old policy.
- *Age.* Sellers must be 65 or older.

Unfortunately, just as very few investors are aware of this opportunity, most people who hold life insurance policies are also unaware that they can sell it. Coventry First, a life settlement company, surveyed 604 seniors citizen in 2016 and reported that **86.1** *percent were not aware of the option to sell their life insurance policies*. This means that the market could be much larger for investors as the public becomes more aware of this opportunity.

History of Fraud & Abuses

One of the reasons that this investment has not gained more popularity is that it has been the subject of fraudulent schemes in the past. Unscrupulous people have ripped off investors through various "Ponzi" schemes in which investors are led to believe that they have purchased shares in a life settlement but their money had not been invested at all. Others have taken advantage of seniors by tricking them into selling valuable life insurance policies for a fraction of the real value.

As with any investment, we must be diligent and skeptical before writing a check. Only work with legitimate life settlement companies with references and long, proven track records. Only buy policies from "A"-rated life insurances companies licensed inside the United States. Get a copy of the life insurance policy and read it before you invest.

Why It Works

So what is the market theory here? In short: a lack of investor demand creates opportunity for high returns. Most investors are not even aware of this opportunity. Many of those who are familiar with this investment vehicle are scared off by the perception of a morality or "ick" factor. Others will not accept the term risk–unknown payoff date.

Investments like this with some undesirable aspects and narrow market appeal create opportunity for those who can accept and see past the "warts." Like the other investments featured in this book, this is not for everyone. It is similar to buying the "ugly" house on the block with broken windows, peeling paint, and overgrown shrubs. The average home buyer turns up her nose and runs away. Investors who can see past the flaws and recognize the value can make above-market returns.

As noted above, most investors who do take the time to understand this opportunity get stuck on the risk associated with trusting the trustee. This is a different situation from mortgage-backed securities ("MBS") to be discussed in Chapter 10. For MBSs like FNMA and GNMA, the trustee is a federal agency, so there is no risk of fraud or a "Ponzi" scheme. Even for private label MBSs, the trustee is typically a well-known bank or large American insurance company. I would not invest in a mortgage-backed security if the mortgages were not held by an extremely trustworthy trustee like a federal agency. This is the main factor that has prevented me from investing in life settlements. I simply can't trust the trustee who is designated to hold the life insurance policy.

This is a situation that seems to call for government intervention. FNMA and GNMA were formed to facilitate funding of mortgages by pooling them and then reselling shares in bonds that are secured by the pool of mortgages. If a government agency were formed to perform the same function for life insurance policies, it would eliminate risk and facilitate the sale of life insurance policies and the resale of fractionated shares to investors.

What Can Go Wrong

1. **Interest Rate Risk**: The resale value of a life settlement will fluctuate as market interest rates change. If prevailing interest rates rise then the resale value of your investment will be reduced.
2. **Extension Risk**: There is no way to accurately predict the term of this investment.
3. **Premiums:** The investor is responsible to make any annual premium payments. Many whole-life insurance policies are "paid in full" at some point, so no further premiums must be paid, but investors must determine what premiums payments (if any) must be paid. Obviously, any premium payments cut away at profits.
4. **Default Risk:** Default risk is extremely low. State regulations ensure that life insurance companies maintain adequate reserves. In the unlikely event of insolvency, states maintain a safety net in the form of guaranty funds to cover policies.
5. **Term Insurance Policies:** Term life insurance expires after a set period of years. The policy is worthless if the insured lives beyond the set term of years. Since there is no way to determine whether the insured will outlive the term of the policy, it is pure speculation to buy a term policy. Experienced, disciplined investors will only consider a term policy if it can be converted into a whole life policy.
6. **Incontestable:** Investors should only consider policies that are "incontestable." Generally, insurance companies may "contest" or challenge payment on an insurance policy that is less than two years old or various reasons including

false information on the application or suicide. Always determine contestability terms before you invest.

7. **Group Policies:** Many people obtain life insurance through a group policy arranged by the insured's employer. These group policies can be purchased, but investor must determine what will happen if the employment is terminated or if the employer simply terminates the policy. Under these circumstances, the investor typically has the right to convert the policy and make the premium payments, but the investor must be aware of all rules and conditions.

8. **Tax Issues:** Life settlements may be purchased through a retirement account, but check with a tax advisor for details in your particular state.

9. **Fraud:** As discussed above, there is a history of fraudulent schemes by life settlement companies, and it is very difficult to sniff out a Ponzi scheme.

Summary of the Pros & Cons

Pros

- ✓ **High potential return:** Potential profit is comparably high.
- ✓ **Diversity:** Life settlements provide a hedge against other investment asset classes such as stocks or bonds. Regardless of the economy, investors hold a contractual right to be paid a predetermined sum of money.
- ✓ **Security:** Life insurance policies are considered to be rock-solid due to government regulations and cash reserve requirements.
- ✓ **Scalability:** There are plenty of opportunities, if your financing allows for multiple purchases.
- ✓ **Stability:** No "market swings" like the stock market or mutual funds.

Cons

- ✓ **Repayment Delays:** The "term" or date of repayment is uncertain.
- ✓ **Morality:** Some investors are uncomfortable with profiting on the death of another.
- ✓ **Illiquid:** This is a long-term investment with an uncertain payoff date.
- ✓ **Capital requirements:** The cost of buying life settlements ranges from $10,000 into the millions.

✓ **Fraud Potential:** Many investors pass on this opportunity due to the history of fraud.

Hungry for More? Source Books, Consultants, Websites, and Sellers

Books:

Bonded Viaticals & Life Settlements, Gloria Wolk

Understanding Life Settlements, David Isaacson

Billion Dollar Blue Print: What Big Banks Don't Want You to Know about Life Settlements, Stephen Gardner (2014)

Testing for Adverse Selection of Life Settlements: The Secondary Market of Life Insurance Policies, Life Settlements Study—2013 University of London; Dr Narayan Naik, Professor of Finance; Joint Chair, Finance Faculty

10

Mortgage-Backed Securities
Ginnie Mae, Fannie Mae, & Freddie Mac

After all of this talk about complex, risky, unfamiliar investment options, here is a safe and easy alternative. Just call your stock broker and buy a mortgage-backed security ("MBS"), such as a Ginnie Mae (GNMA), which is guaranteed by the United States government. It is a bond, so it generates a stream of income and is guaranteed to return your principal over a period of years. The bond is backed by a huge pool of mortgages, and as the debtors pay their mortgages, a piece of the interest and principal is distributed to you as a bond holder on an amortized basis. If you just hold the bond until the end of its term, you are guaranteed to get all of the interest and all of your principal back. No risk. No work, no specialized knowledge required.

So, what's the catch? There is always a catch! Investments like this with low risk always offer low reward. In the current market, an MBS with an anticipated paydown period of three to six years will only earn about 3 percent interest. You can earn a slightly higher yield if you extend the term out for a longer period of years.

The risks are very low. Your principal and interest payments will be safely paid to you. There is no risk of default if you buy GNMA bonds because they are guaranteed by the federal government. If a debtor defaults on one or more of the mortgages that are bundled together in your bond, it has no effect on you—the government incurs the loss. The only questions:

1. When will all of your principal be returned?
2. Will you miss out on higher interest rates while you are waiting for your bond to be repaid?

The term of the bond is flexible because it depends on repayment of the mortgages that make up the trust. If many people pay off their mortgage early, through sales or refinancing for example, your investment will be returned more quickly. If the debtors do not pay back their mortgages early, your investment funds will be paid back to you a bit more slowly, but you will receive interest payments until you are fully paid off.

Summary Points

1. **No Specialized Knowledge:** Just call your stock broker or financial advisor.
2. **Reasonable Capital Requirement:** Bonds can be bought for as low as $1,000.
3. **Scalability:** Yes. There is an enormous supply of bonds for investors.
4. **Liquidity:** The bonds can be sold, but depending on the current market interest rate, your bonds may be worth more or less than you paid.
5. **No Barriers to Entry:** Just call your broker or financial advisor.

Risks

The main risks relate to how interest rates may move in the free market. If you do not sell your MBS bond, regardless of how interest rates fluctuate in the general market, you are guaranteed to receive your principal and interest when the bond matures. The interest rate is "fixed" for these bonds, so they will not fluctuate up or down with the market. This is favorable when prevailing interest rates are falling in the market, since you will continue to earn your "fixed rate interest." The concern is that if market interest rates rise sharply, you are still locked in at your "fixed rate" of interest, and you will be anxious to get your money back so that you can reinvest in new bonds at a higher rate of interest.

Three Possible Scenarios:

1. **Interest Rates Rise.** Fewer debtors will refinance their mortgages, so it will take longer for bonds to be paid off, and investors will have to wait longer to take advantage of the higher interest rates by buying new bonds.

2. **Interest Rates Decrease.** More debtors will pay off their mortgages by refinancing at a lower rate, so bond investors will be paid off sooner.
3. **Interest Rates Stay the Same.** The MBS bonds will be paid off as expected, and the investors will reinvest at about the same rate.

There is no risk of default for GNMA bonds because they guaranteed by the full faith and credit of the United Sates. As discussed below, there is some risk of default for other types of MBS bonds depending on which agency or entity issued the bonds.

Some Terminology
Here are some terms and acronyms that are commonly thrown around:

ABS: Asset-Backed Security is a bond that is secured by an asset such as a mortgage. An MBS is a type of Asset Backed Security.

MBS: Mortgage-Backed security, like GNMA or FNMA.

RMBS: A mortgage-backed security that holds mortgages on residential properties such as single and two-family homes.

CMBS: A mortgage-backed security that holds mortgages on commercial properties such as office buildings, stores, and apartment buildings.

Principal: Borrowed funds.

Interest: Money paid to a lender for the use of borrowed funds.

Market Rate Interest: The prevailing interest rate for a given duration as set by trading on a market.

Tranche: French word for "slice." Often used in discussing how MBS pools are sliced up into different parts for distribution of payments.

Securitization: Pooling various types of debt such as mortgages, and selling the cash flow to investors as bonds. The type of debt (such as mortgages or unsecured credit card debt) impacts the risk of the bonds

Average Life: Average predicted period in which a debt is repaid through amortization.

How is this Done?

Thousands of mortgages are grouped together into a trust, and as the debtors make monthly payments on the mortgages, the funds are pooled and distributed to the bond holders in accordance with the term of the MBS security. The mortgage payments include interest and principal, so as payments are collected and distributed each month, a portion of the principal is returned to the investor along with the accrued interest.

This continuous return of principal has advantages and disadvantages. Investors like to get principal back early when interest rates are rising, because the funds can be reinvested into a new higher-yielding bond. But when interest rates are falling, the returned funds must be invested into a new bond with a lower yield.

Also, as the principal is returned in small portions each month, it usually sweeps into a money market fund (which earns very low interest) until it accumulates enough to buy another bond. This may seem petty, but the uninvested funds are not working for you, and they reduce your interest income. Other types of bonds such as municipal bonds or corporate bonds do not share this problem because all principal is paid back at once at the end of the bond term, so the investor accrues interest for the entire term.

Just Call Your Broker

Buying a MBS bond is very easy. Just call your financial advisor or broker and ask to speak with a broker who specializes in bonds. The process to buy is similar to buying a stock. It gets a little more complicated when deciding *which* MBS bond to buy because the bonds differ based on what entity issues the bonds and how the MBS is structured.

Premiums & Discounts

New bonds are issued at "par," which means price is equal to the the face value of the bond. Like any other bond or security, MBS bonds may be resold and traded in the secondary market. If you are buying a bond in the secondary market, it may be priced at par, at a discount or at a premium based on how interest rates have changed since the bond was issued.

Par: If interest rates in the marketplace have not changed since the bond was issued, the bond will likely trade at close to par, which is the face value of the bond.

Discount: When market interest rates increase, it reduces the value of bonds that were previously issued with lower interest rates. Why would an investor buy your older bond yielding 2 percent when similar new bonds are being issued with a 3 percent yield? The only way to attract a buyer would be to discount the price so the effective yield would match the current market rates.

Premium: On the other hand, if interest rates drop in the market, then your higher yielding "old" bonds will increase in market value. This is because the market will adjust the value of your bond to reflect that it accrues interest higher than the market rate. Investors would rather buy your higher-yielding bonds than the new lower-yielding bonds, and they will pay more for it.

Principal Paydown: Of course, the price will also reflect how much of the bond has already been paid off. Principal and interest payments are collected and distributed to bond holders each month, so as the bond ages, the principal due on the bond is paid down and the value of the bond is reduced.

Keep in mind that these **price fluctuations only apply if you sell your bond**. As long as you hold the bond to the end of its term (to"maturity"), you will be paid all of the principal and interest. You will see a "paper loss" or "paper gain" on your monthly brokerage statements, which list the current market value of each bond, but you will not incur the gain or loss unless you sell the bond before it matures.

Types of MBS Bonds

MBS bonds are created or "issued" by a variety of government and private entities. Characteristics and risks of the MBS vary depending on the issuer, so it is critical for investors to be familiar with each type of MBS. There are four general types of mortgage backed securities:

1. **Government National Mortgage ("GNMA" or "Ginnie Mae)** is an agency of the federal government created to ensure that mortgage loans are available throughout the country. GNMA bonds are guaranteed by the "full faith and credit" of the United States Treasury, so even if every mortgage in the pool were to default, the investors would still be paid in full. The only down-side is that the bonds are sold in $25,000 minimum increments, as opposed to the other MBS bonds that are offered in $1,000 increments. GNMA bonds can be bought for less than $25,000 on the secondary market as they are paid down and closer to maturity. Individual investors can also buy a GNMA mutual fund or ETF, but they differ significantly from an individual bond.
2. **Federal National Mortgage Association ("FNMA" or "Fannie Mae")** is a publicly owned corporation that was formed by the federal government to

increase and support the secondary market for home mortgages. It buys mortgages from banks. It is also not a government agency, and the bonds are not *explicitly* guaranteed by the US Treasury, so they are considered slightly riskier than GNMA.

Although it is not a governmental agency, it was formed by the federal government and its bonds are guaranteed by FNMA as the issuer. It is widely considered that FNMA is "too big to fail," so investors generally believe that the federal government would not allow it to default on its MBS bonds. Accordingly, the market deems these bonds to be "***implicitly***" guaranteed by the fed and extremely secure, so these bonds yield just slightly more than fully guaranteed GNMA bonds. FNMA Bonds are issued in $1,000 increments.

3. **Federal Home Loan Mortgage Corporation ("FHLMC" or "Freddie Mac")** is also a publicly owned corporation that was formed by the federal government to increase the home mortgage market. Like FNMA, Freddie Mac is widely considered to be "too big to fail," so the public considers the bonds to be extremely secure. Freddie Mac bonds are also issued in $1,000 increments.

4. **Private mortgage-backed securities.** Large financial institutions like Goldman Sachs and J.P. Morgan Chase create private mortgage-backed securities, based on pools of mortgages that are held in a trust for bond holders. The government has no involvement, so there is no direct or implied government guarantee, and these bonds accordingly carry a higher yield. These "private label" bonds may be offered with insurance that greatly reduces risk.

Variations on How MBS Bonds Are Structured:

Here is where it gets a bit more complicated. Creative financial companies have devised ways to repackage MBS bonds to better fit investors' needs.

"Pass-through" MBS: This is the standard straightforward type of MBS. The issuer, GNMA for example, collects payments from a large batch of mortgages and "passes through" the collected principal and interest to the bondholders. Funds are collected from three sources: monthly payments of principal, monthly payments of interest, and prepaid principal (when the homeowner refinances or sells the home.) The bond term extends until the last mortgage is fully paid off, so the date of final payment is uncertain. As explained above, the long and uncertain repayment term is undesirable for some investors who wish to avoid prepayment and extension risk.

Collateralized Mortgage Obligations (CMOs) are designed to improve pass-through mortgage-backed securities by making repayment more predictable. CMO sponsors bundle together a bunch of mortgage-backed securities and repackage them with a prioritized order of payment. Cash flow is segregated into different bond classes known as "tranches," which is a French term for slice. Each tranche is assigned an order of priority for repayment. The tranches are designed to provide investors with more predictable repayments.

For example, a pool of 30-year mortgages could be broken up into four tranches with different payoff expectations. Bonds issued for the first tranche may have an expected repayment term (or "average life") of five years, and all of the mortgage payments of principal and some of the interest from the entire pool of mortgages would be directed to these first tranche bond holders until they are paid off. This creates a short-term bond, which reduces risks and accordingly would carry a lower interest rate. Once the first tranche is paid off, then all mortgage principal payments will be directed to the second tranche until it is fully paid off. The other three tranches may have "average lives" of 10, 15, and 30 years and would accrue higher interest rates to reflect the longer terms.

Some CMOs have a dozen or more tranches, and they can be structured in limitless ways to create tranches to perform in different predictable ways to suit different investors.

Real Estate Mortgage Investment Conduits ("REMICs" or "Conduits") are similar to CMOs but have more complex tranches. Instead of just slicing tranches up by the order of repayment, REMICs also sort mortgages by risk. Some tranches include only the highest-quality, lowest-risk mortgages, and others include the lowest-quality, highest-risk mortgages. Investors can choose the quality that best suits their need. Of course, the higher-risk, low-quality tranches yield more, and the lower-risk, high-quality tranches yield a lower interest rate.

Yes, These Are "Derivatives," But Don't Be Afraid:

An MBS is considered to be a "derivative" investment because it is "derived" from a different investment. It is a bond that is derived or created from a pool of mortgages. Many investors have a vague conception that derivatives are bad. This reputation was generated through a series of financial scandals that involved complex and misleading derivative investments. Not all derivatives are bad, and government MBS bonds are widely considered to be a safe income investment.

This diagram is an example of how a CMO may be structured:

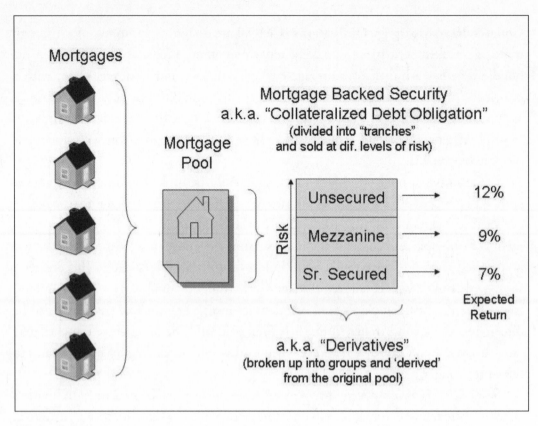

Source: Wikipedia.

Commissions & Fees

Buyers generally do not pay a commission or fee to invest in an MBS. Brokers make money by buying large batches of MBS bonds and then reselling them at a higher price.

Structuring a "Ladder" of bonds:

A common technique for managing interest rate risk is to build a portfolio of bonds with different maturity terms, so that a portion of your principal is always invested in higher-yielding long term bonds and a portion of your bonds is always close to maturity, so the funds can be reinvested at the current interest rates. For example:

20% of Bond Portfolio	10-Year Term Bonds
20% of Bond Portfolio	8-Year Term Bonds
20% of Bond Portfolio	6-Year Term Bonds
20% of Bond Portfolio	4-Year Term Bonds
20% of Bond Portfolio	2-Year Term Bonds

No one can consistently predict the fluctuations of interest rates, so this ladder approach allows you to diversify your bond portfolio with both long- and short-term bonds. When the 2-year bonds mature, the funds are reinvested into a new 10-year bond. And when the 4-year bonds mature, once again, the money is reinvested in new 10-year bonds. By following this process, you will build a portfolio of 10-year bonds (earning higher, 10-year yields) maturing every 2 years to be reinvested into high-yielding 10-year bonds.

Why It Works

No one is going to "beat the market" buying MBS bonds. This is designed as a safe portion of a portfolio. Income-seeking investors are attracted to MBS bonds because they yield more than bank CDs and because of the federal government's explicit (for GNMA) and implicit (FNMA & FHLMC) guarantees. The federal government has determined that the overall economy is at least partially driven by homeownership, so these agencies were created to insure that mortgage loans are readily available throughout the country. The sale of MBS bonds provides funding for the nationwide mortgage market, so there is always a strong supply of bonds for investors, and the federal government will undoubtedly protect this market from default.

What Can Go Wrong:

1. **Interest Rates Risk**: A bond's resale value will fluctuate as market interest rates change. A bond's value has an *inverse relationship* to market interest rates. If prevailing interest rates rise higher than your bond's rate, the resale value of your bond will be reduced. On the other hand, your bond's resale value will increase if market interest rates fall. In any event, an investor who holds a bond for its full term will receive the principal and interest rate paid in full, regardless of prevailing market interest rates.
2. **Prepayment Risk**: MBS bonds may be paid off early if the underlying mortgages are paid off earlier than expected. This occurs more often as prevailing interest rate are falling. The MBS bond will be paid off earlier, and the investor will have to reinvest, possibly at a lower yield.
3. **Extension Risk**: This is the opposite of "prepayment risk." MBS bonds may be paid off more slowly than anticipated if the underlying mortgages are paid off

later than expected. This occurs more often as prevailing interest rates are rising and the mortgage debtors are less likely to refinance or pay off the mortgage. The MBS bond will be paid off later, delaying the investor's ability to reinvest in new higher-yielding bonds.

4. **Delayed Reinvestment Risk**: As small portions of the investor's principal are returned each month, they may sit idle for a period of time before being reinvested, and they may have to be reinvested at a lower yield.

5. **Default Risk:** There is no risk of default for GNMA bonds, which are guaranteed by the full faith and credit of the United States Treasury. Although there is a technical risk for default for bonds issued by FNMA & FHLMC, they are considered to be extremely secure. MBS bonds issued by private banks and financial companies are subject to possible default.

Summary of the Pros & Cons

Pros

- ✓ **Diversity:** Mortgage-backed bonds provide diversity from stocks and general economic swings.
- ✓ **Security:** There is no risk of default for GNMA bonds, which are guaranteed by the full faith and credit of the United States Treasury, and extremely low risk of default for Fannie Mae and Freddie Mac bonds, which the market considers to have an implied guarantee.
- ✓ **Scalability:** Almost unlimited supply of MBS bonds.
- ✓ **Stability:** No major "market swings" like the stock market or mutual funds.

Cons

- ✓ **Low Yield:** Due to the low-risk nature of MBS bonds, the yield is low.

Hungry for More? Source Books, Consultants, Websites, and Sellers

Books:

Mortgage-Backed Securities, Justin Adams

The Handbook of Mortgage-Backed Securities, Frank Fabozzi

Investing in Bonds For Dummies, Russell Wild

11

Morality of Investing in Debt

Whether we like it or not, morality issues are an unavoidable part of investing in debt. Many of the clients and investors I have known have admitted to having morality issues, and I must admit that I have occasionally struggled with this in my role as a tax lien foreclosure attorney.

No matter how you cut it, debt investors make money on the hardship of other people. I have taken thousands of calls from desperate owners seeking more time or help. One elderly man shot himself on the day of his scheduled eviction. Another woman called several times expressing concern over where her many cats would live after she was evicted. Another man burned his home down on the day of eviction. We hear heartwrenching stories of how their great-grandfather built the house many years ago and the family just can't lose it. Some people continue to call and write to me *years* after the foreclosure was completed. There is no escaping the dark side of these investments.

People seem to deal with this morality issue in different ways—but *everyone* must deal with it. I suppose that there may be some people who are so blinded by greed that this issue does not present a problem, but then again, ***that*** is their way of dealing with it. They focus solely on the money that they are making and do not think about the effects. I suspect that this is a rare individual. Most people, whether they admit it or not, have some pangs of anxiety over this issue.

Most people try to avoid facing this problem through rationalizations. I refer to these as rationalizations because they do not really address or resolve the morality issue. They are just ways of escaping it.

They Brought This upon Themselves

The most common rationalization is that the delinquent tax payers brought this problem upon themselves by failing to pay their debts. This is, of course, true, but it often doesn't make them less sympathetic. Many good, hardworking people find themselves in financial trouble due to illness, the economy, or the death of a spouse. Many elderly people have found that despite working there entire adult lives, they simply cannot afford to live in their home after retirement. This is especially true of widows and widowers who lose the social security or pension income of a deceased spouse. Sure, you can say that their failure to earn enough money is not *your* fault, but it doesn't make it any easier.

Obviously, financial hardship does not necessarily lead to foreclosure. Most people sell their property and move to a more affordable location if they can no longer afford their home. Some people, unfortunately, do not face the problems they find themselves in. Whether it be denial, ignorance, or incapacity to deal with problems, there are many people who lose their home because they simply do not take the right steps to keep their home or at least to salvage the valuable equity in the property.

To simply say that the delinquent property owners brought the situation upon themselves, or failed to respond to address the problem, is true, but it does not alter the fact that people who invest in debt are profiting from the misfortune of others. Again, I am not suggesting that this is a bad or wrong thing to do. I simply wish to point out that this issue exists and shouldn't be ignored.

The Creation and Collection of Debt Is Beneficial to Debtors, Creditors, and the Public

It is easy to sympathize with debtors and villainize creditors, but imagine a system in which debt could not be enforced or collected: there would be no lenders and no loans. Without loans (and a system to efficiently collect them), only people with vast liquid wealth could afford to buy a home, invest in real estate, or expand a business. Debt is the lubricant in the economic engine. Accordingly, public policy favors the creation and orderly collection of debt because it serves the overall public welfare.

Borrowers benefit by having access to cash through an active and competitive loan market. If the borrower eventually cannot repay the loan, he or she simply loses the collateral that was pledged to secure the loan. Unlike in other societies, our debtors are not physically punished. Our society has no debtor's prison. Upon default, the debtor simply loses the collateral that was pledged to secure the loan.

The overall economy benefits by having more buyers available to purchase products with easily obtained debt. Each purchase recycles through the economy over and over in the form of sales taxes, wages paid to sales clerks, wholesalers and distributors, etc.

Lenders obviously benefit through interest earned on repaid debt.

If I Don't Do It, Someone Else Will

I did not invent any of the debt investment techniques discussed in this book. People have been investing in these for years. As we entered and emerged from the Great Recession there has been enormous demand for alternative debt investments. Whether you invest in debt or not, someone else will, but investors must ask themselves whether they want to be the person who engages in this.

The Answer Is: There Is No Answer . . .

It *is* what it *is*. I cannot offer any way to escape the morality issue. I don't believe that there is any neat and easy way around it. This dilemma is just part of debt investing. Obviously, I personally do not think these investors are bad people or that investing in debt is a bad thing. This is just a part of the business that must be dealt with.

Some of the investment options discussed in this book present more of a morality problem than others. For example, peer-to-peer and "White Knight" rescues are typically seen as helping someone who is in financial need—although the investor still seeks to make a tidy profit based on the financial need of another. For those who are uncomfortable with this issue, consider the options that are less directly connected with debtors, such as annuities, sheriff's sales, and publicly traded stocks and bonds.

12

True Story!

One of the best ways to learn about any subject is through anecdotes of success and hardship. Stories about other investors' experiences are much more interesting than memorizing rules, and true stories tend to stick with us. As children, we all learned about morality and religion through parables and stories. Law schools teach the law through case studies in which we study old cases and argue about how to apply the lessons to different fact patterns.

Whenever I run into another foreclosure attorney, we inevitably share a story or two: "You won't believe this one" or "Wait till you hear this one." I've collected and summarized a few of the more interesting scenarios that I have experienced, either personally or through a client. Reading these might offer good advice, as well as situations to be wary of.

1. *The Rip Van Winkle Eviction*

A client called me and asked if I'd handle an eviction for him. He explained there were two unusual factors: a different attorney handled the foreclosure and the final judgment had been entered over eight years earlier. The long delay was highly unusual. Most clients are very anxious to line up an eviction as quickly as possible so they can start to rehab and sell the property. My first thought was that he had been renting the property back to the former owners, which would complicate the eviction a bit, but he assured me that he had not entered into any lease and never accepted any rent from the family.

So why had he waited eight years, and why does he want to evict them now? The client explained that when he had completed the foreclosure process eight earlier, he personally visited the house to try to negotiate a friendly "cash-for-keys" arrangement to gain possession of the house, which was in a tough inner-city neighborhood. The former owner of the property answered the door, and when my client introduced himself, the former owner very calmly told him to "wait right here while I get my gun." Of course, my client took the hint and left, having full faith that the occupant meant exactly what he said.

I understood why he left, but I was still puzzled why he waited so long to do anything. This is where my client had made a mistake. He had been buying tax liens in his own name, rather than through a corporation or LLC, and he has a very uncommon name, making him easily found by anyone with Internet access. He didn't want this defendant to show up at his house, so my client elected to just sit back and wait.

Now, eight years later, he was ready to retire and wanted to cash out, so he came to me to solve the problem. We conveyed the property into an LLC and began the process for a sheriff's eviction. The family, who was still residing in the house, opposed the eviction initially, claiming that they had no notice of the foreclosure. When I produced proof of service and multiple mailed notices, they claimed that they were entitled to stay because they had repaired the roof and did a bit of painting inside the house over the past eight years.

Fortunately, the judge agreed that whatever the family had spent to maintain the house over the past eight years was much less than the value of occupying the house without having to pay any rent or property taxes during those years. The judge gave them an extension to move out, and they vacated without incident.

The lesson here is not to pursue foreclosures in your own name. Investing through a corporation or LLC makes it appear much less personal and helps to maintain your privacy. This story also highlights the risk involved in visiting the subject property. As discussed in a few of the other chapters, I recommend trying to reach "cash-for-keys" deals, but personal one-on-one contact is not for everyone.

2. Eviction Horror Stories

Most evictions proceed without incident. Many times the occupants even move out before the eviction date to avoid being physically moved out by the sheriff's officers. Some evictions, however, turn tragic, and it is important for investors to keep in mind that these investments aren't just about money. Real people are involved, and the foreclosure can often be more than they can handle.

In one of my cases many years ago, the defendant did not oppose the foreclosure or contact me in any way. When the eviction date eventually arrived and the sheriff's officer knocked on the door, the former owner shot himself. The officers heard the shot, broke in, and rushed the man to a hospital, where he was saved. We learned that he was a handicapped veteran. Fortunately, his friends and family raised money for him, and he was able to get his home back.

Just last year, a natural gas explosion destroyed a house and killed the occupant just two days before an eviction. Again, the former owner did not oppose the foreclosure or contact me in any way, but investigators believe that he intentionally created the explosion to destroy the house and commit suicide.

As I wrote this book, we encountered yet another horrible eviction. The owner of the property did not speak English very well, but throughout the foreclosure process he repeatedly advised my office and my client that his "daughter was taking care of it." Despite his repeated assurances, the lien was not paid off, and the foreclosure was completed. On the date of the eviction, my client, the sheriff's officer, and the moving crew found the owner planting in his garden, which obviously is not what he would be doing if he understood that he was about to be evicted. Again, the owner explained that he gave his daughter funds to "take care of it," and he led my client and the sheriff's officer around the corner to his daughter's home. Upon arriving, the daughter was found to have committed suicide, and there was no sign of what happened to the money that was to be used to stop the foreclosure.

Fortunately, the owner was able to raise more money, and my client was cooperative in allowing the family to get the property back.

These types of tragic incidents are relatively rare, but they are always on my mind as an eviction date draws near. Investors who want to participate in foreclosures must be aware of this risk.

3. The Arsonist Hoarder

I truly hate to see any of my clients run into bad luck and suffer a loss. Most of my clients are corporate investors or experienced individuals who can bounce back from a loss, but I still cringe when I see misfortune strike a client through no fault of their own. I've represented a client from the Atlantic City area for a few years, and we have struck up a friendship. He treats everyone with fairness and respect and is a really good guy, so this story bothers me *almost* as much as it hurt him.

This client had a tax lien on a vacant house in a run-down, depressed area near Atlantic City. We completed the foreclosure, and he took over the house. It had been vacant for years with broken windows, no heat, and frozen pipes. Worse yet, the house had been owned by a hoarder, so it was literally FULL of junk. He told me that he could not even open the front door more than one-third of the way because newspapers and assorted trash were piled up everywhere. This is not uncommon in foreclosed homes.

The foreclosure had been unopposed and the family had moved out long ago, but as soon as we had a dumpster delivered and he started to clean the house out, the former owner ran to court and asked for an emergent stay of eviction. Apparently, the former owners still lived in the neighborhood and saw the dumpster being delivered. I opposed the request on the obvious grounds that they had moved out years ago, so they weren't being *evicted*. They asked the Judge to give them sole possession of the house for 30 days so they could remove some personal belongings. Once a foreclosure is completed and we have ownership and possession, it is never a good thing to give it back, so I argued that we should retain possession. I suggested that the family could take anything they want as the house is being cleaned out over the next few days, but my client should maintain sole control and possession of the house. Unfortunately, the judge saw it differently. The judge explained that he saw no harm in allowing the former owner to regain possession for 30 days, so he ordered my client to remove the locks and stay away for a month.

The former owners spent a day or two removing a few items, and then the house burned down to the ground. Instead of obtaining a house to rehab and resell, my client now had a low-value lot with a pile of ashes and debris in a distressed neighborhood. There is always a risk of the property being damaged or destroyed during a foreclosure process, and it is difficult to obtain fire insurance on a structure when you don't have full control and possession of it.

4. *The Substitute Building Inspector*

Many years ago, my brother-in-law and I bought a foreclosed vacant house from a bank. We had limited access to the house, but we did as much prepurchase diligence as possible to determine the condition of the house and estimate the repair costs. It was a tight deal with no potential for a huge profit, but the house was across the street from a rental property that we owned, so we decided to make the deal.

As soon as we closed, I applied for all necessary permits, and the borough building and plumbing inspectors walked through the house before issuing permits to begin the rehab. We had our contractors lined up, so as soon as the permits were issued, full work crews descended upon the small house replacing the windows, installing vinyl siding, painting, and repairing every square foot of the house, which had been vacant for years and was in very bad shape.

Then the project came to a costly stop. Unbeknownst to me, the senior building inspector had been away on vacation when the permits had been issued by an inspector who had been filling in for him. When he returned and discovered our rehab, the inspector immediately shut down all work and placed a bright red sticker in the front window, without even bothering to call me. When my contractor advised me of the shutdown, I called the inspector to inquire, but he was too busy to return my calls—for four days! When I finally reached him, he explained that he had been away, and the permits should not have been issued in his opinion without an engineering report to confirm that the house was still viable after having been vacant for so long.

Now I was disappointed by this, but it was a rational position that I could understand. Keep in mind that I had already sunk thousands of dollars into rehab costs, which would be entirely wasted if the house had to be taken down. So maybe *disappointed* is an understatement, but I was confident that the house was structurally sound.

I had an engineer inspect the house on an emergent time frame, which of course costed extra, and I filed the engineer's report confirming that the house was structurally sound. By now, the project had been delayed almost three weeks, and I just needed the inspector to review the engineer's report and remove his red sticker from my house. I naively assumed that the building inspector would respond quickly, since I had done nothing wrong. The inspector did accept my engineering report and removed his red sticker, allowing the rehab to be completed, but he took an additional three weeks to get around to it. The engineering report and delays added about $4,000 to our costs.

What lesson can be gleaned from this? Inspectors and the permit process vary in each town. Some are very cooperative and helpful, and others seem to go out of their way to make life difficult. Of course, all building codes and laws must be met, but some inspectors can take a hostile approach, causing needless and unfair delays. There is no way to avoid this risk, so you must budget for unforeseen delays.

5. *The Belmar Beach House and the Italian Heir*

Sometimes we cannot locate the owner of a property upon which we are foreclosing. This is a problem, because we have to serve notice of the foreclosure to the property owner. Court rules address this problem by allowing "constructive" notice to be published in the local newspapers, and notice to be posted on the door of the subject house, if a full and diligent effort is made to locate and serve the owner.

A few years ago, I foreclosed on a vacant rundown house in a Belmar, a beautiful beachside town along the Jersey Shore. The tax lien was over five years old, and the house had been vacant for at least that long. We could not locate and serve the owner, so we inquired with neighbors and the tax collector, and we were advised that the owner had passed away years ago. Of course, we checked "surrogate" records to hunt for heirs, but there was no record of the estate in New Jersey. Having run into a dead end, we published notice in the local newspapers and posted notice on the door, and we proceeded to final judgment.

My client wisely obtained a title insurance policy to protect his investment and then proceeded to tear down the small old house and built a beautiful new beach house. Just as my client entered a contract to sell the new house, we received a motion to vacate our foreclosure. An heir of the former owner, who lived in Italy, argued that he was not served and he wanted the property back—with the beautiful new house!

My client's title insurance policy protected him from this risk, and the title company retained me to defend my foreclosure. The heir argued that if I had searched harder, I could have found him in Italy, and then he would have paid off the tax lien and prevented the foreclosure. During the foreclosure process, the tax collector had told me that there was a property management service based in New York that was managing the property for a short period of time, years ago. We contacted that property manager and served the foreclosure papers on it as an extra step, hoping to reach the owner, but we received no response. The heir argued that we could have made a better effort pursuing that lead and it might have led to the heir's former address in England, which (*he argued*) could have led us to the heir's current address in Italy.

Thankfully, the judge threw the heir's case out of court, ruling that we had made a reasonable effort and we were not required to be clairvoyant in discovering people who have left their property vacant for years. The lesson here is to always get title insurance before rehabilitating or replacing a foreclosed property.

6. *Dead Pit Bulls, Drugs, Porn, and Counterfeit Jeans*

You may be surprised by what you find in foreclosed homes. Whether you invest in defaulted mortgages, tax liens, sheriff's sale properties, or bank REOs, you get the property "as is." Sometimes, when you are lucky, the property has been cleared out, but most of the time, it will take a dumpster or two to clear out the contents. People who have lost their home usually just take what they can and leave everything else behind, including food in the refrigerator, old furniture, unwanted clothing, and decades of accumulated junk.

I've often been surprised by the things that are left behind. I've found a rifle, family photo albums, unopened gifts, complete sets of china, personal tax records, and even cars. It is common to find drug paraphernalia, like baggies and pipes. The basement of one old house was stacked with pornography VHS tapes and duplication equipment, used to copy and resell the porn tapes.

On one occasion, I foreclosed on a house that had been used to make and sell counterfeit designer jeans. There were shelves of jeans for sale in the front living room, and a bedroom was stacked with boxes of cheap jeans alongside bags of counterfeit designer labels. Apparently, the former owner was an entrepreneur who had to leave in a hurry.

By far, I was most disturbed by what I found in an old vacant brownstone in a tough neighborhood of Jersey City, New Jersey. There was a temporary police trailer set up on the block, so the house was clearly on a high crime street, but I was encouraged by the police presence. Criminal activity tends to migrate into a different neighborhood when the police set up a presence on the street.

It was late summer and the house was closed up, so it felt like an oven inside. I immediately noticed two dog cages with decomposing pit bulls locked inside, and a third dead dog by the back door. They had been there for a long time, and their skeletons were partially exposed. As I was a dog lover, it made me sick. There were several boxes of small plastic bags that are used to sell drugs, so I assume the house was occupied by a drug dealer who, for one reason or another, was unable to return to the house. I decided that I wanted no part of trying to rehab this house, so I had a crew clean it out and sold it "as is" to a local investor.

7. The Lost Art of Embroidery

This story is another example of how we don't always know what we are getting. A client came to me with a tax lien on a lot that had no street frontage. The lot included a small commercial building in a residential neighborhood in Hudson County, New Jersey, but the lot was completely surrounded by houses. Access to my client's lot was limited to an easement through a narrow alley between two of the houses that surround the building.

My client was a large institutional tax lien investment company and did not discover this situation before buying the tax lien. It identified the lot as being in a residential area and just assumed it was a typical house with direct street access. A couple of years after having bought the lien, my client discovered that the lien was on this commercial building surrounded by houses. Apparently, decades earlier a family owned an embroidery business in the commercial building and built houses all around the commercial building for family and key employees. The lots were eventually subdivided and sold off to separate owners, but of course the physical layout remained.

Lack of adequate street access is a severe problem for a commercial building, but this was only part of the problem. After we completed the foreclosure, we discovered that the building was almost entirely filled with a large steel embroidery machine, which of course would have to be removed in order to sell or rent the building. The machinery had to be cut apart and removed in small pieces through the narrow alley between the neighboring houses.

8. The Sovereign Princess's Tax Exemption

Over the years, having seen thousands of foreclosure files, I have run into some very unusual individuals. One lady had a particularly odd view of society. She sent me letters and filed papers in court insisting that she is royalty of her own sovereign nation that is separate and apart from the United States. As a separate nation, she reasoned, she is not subject to municipal, state, or federal taxes. She also asserted that the New Jersey court system had no jurisdiction or power over her.

Fortunately, I never had the pleasure of meeting her in person. She appeared in court to delay the eviction, but the judge allowed me to argue the case by telephone. She referred to herself in the third person. asserting her status as tax exempt royalty. The judge gave her some extra time to move out.

9. The Sweet Smell of Success?

At the peak of the Great Recession, one of my clients came across a vacant warehouse that was about to be sold at sheriff's sale due to a mortgage foreclosure. The market for empty warehouse space plummeted during the recession, so we thought we could buy this warehouse for a low price, and we would generate nice rental income once the recession eventually came to an end.

Of course, we did the best we could on our presale due diligence, but the warehouse had no windows, and we could not get inside. It was a refrigerated warehouse that had been used by a food distributor, but it had been vacant for years, so we assumed the worst-case scenario—that the refrigeration units were dead. That was OK with us because we planned to rent it out as a typical warehouse without refrigeration.

We celebrated when we won the bid, and I had no problem contacting the former owner and getting his keys. In fact, he met us at the warehouse the day after the sheriff's sale. He only wanted to take his desk. As we entered the warehouse for the first time, we were hit with a strong odor of rotting food. The front of the warehouse was office space, so we had no idea how bad it was until the former owner left with his desk and we ventured back into the warehouse. The odor was almost unbearable. We correctly anticipated that the refrigeration equipment would be shot, but it had not occurred to either of us that the space would be stacked twenty-five feet high with formerly frozen, now-rotten food. We had literally tons of shrimp patties, turkey burgers, chicken wings, and all sorts of other rotten food products. We assumed that most of the goods would have been sold off at a liquidation sale before the building was vacated, but we were very mistaken. My partner spent weeks there with day labor filling dumpster after dumpster. When the rotten food was finally all removed, a different crew of cleaning people toiled for days with sprays and brushes to kill the bacteria and odor.

The rest of the rehab project went as expected, and after carrying it empty for a few years waiting for the market to recover, we found a tenant and are enjoying a nice rental income. The moral to this story is that there are ALWAYS surprises in foreclosure properties. We just hope for small surprises rather than large ones.

10. Resurrection & Reforeclosure of the Grave Stone Shop

About ten years ago, I completed a tax lien foreclosure on a small lot with a tiny shack-like office that had been used to sell grave stones. The owner, of course, did not live there and had very sporadic hours of operation. In fact, the business appeared to be closed. We ran a skip trace to discovered the owner's home address and had him personally served at his home.

After final judgment had been entered, the former owner hired an attorney and challenged the foreclosure, claiming that he was not properly served with the complaint. I produced an affidavit of service that indicated that he was in fact personally served at the condo where he resided, but he persisted that he had not received any notices, and he suggested that perhaps the process server delivered the summons to a neighbor by mistake. My client and I did not believe him because I had also *mailed* notices to his condo and to the grave stone shop, and we even posted notice on the door of the shop. The owner had a sympathetic story involving some severe illnesses and he had funds to pay off the lien, so my client, who was a local investor, agreed to vacate the final judgment and allow him to pay off the tax lien.

Four years later, the same client came to me with a new tax lien on the same grave stone shop. He reminded me of our history with the property, and we started to foreclose again. Like déjà vu, we completed the long foreclosure process with several notices being delivered, mailed, and posted at the subject's shop and also at the owner's condo. As soon as we obtained and mailed out the final judgment, he filed another motion to vacate the judgment, using the same attorney, again swearing that he had not received notice of the foreclosure. Again, he asserted that he was suffering with some severe illnesses, but this time, he admitted that he lacked funds to pay off the lien.

This time around, my client was less tolerant, and we aggressively litigated the issue. We filed papers in court, reminding the judge that this defendant had made the same arguments a few years earlier and that we settled. We also obtained statements from neighbors on both sides of the owner's condo, to establish that they had not been served in error, as the defendant suggested. The judge saw right through the defendant's ruse and denied his motion to vacate judgment. My client resold the property for a small profit but had to arrange to get rid of dozens of sample grave stones that the defendant abandoned at the lot.

Some of these stories are comical, and most are sad, but they provide some insight into investing in distressed debt. By sharing these experiences, I hope that the ideas and principles discussed in this book will be made more real and concrete. For every "home run" or success story, there is also a nightmare scenario. Even if you are careful, you will still run into snags and problems, but with experience and discipline, you should experience more positives than negatives.

In Conclusion . . .

Thank you for taking the time to read this book. I hope that you enjoyed learning about these alternative ways to invest, and I hope I've left you with an interest in learning more about these subjects. This is my fourth book, and, although it was challenging, I enjoyed the opportunity to introduce this information to you. There has been very little written about most of these investments, and I hope that you found each chapter to be a clear and concise introduction to each investment concept.

These complex alternative investments are clearly not meant for novices or investors with small investment portfolios. Small investors and beginners are better suited for stocks, mutual funds, and rental properties. That is exactly how I started, and I've encouraged my college-aged children to start the same way.

Alternative investments such as these are intended for more seasoned investors with large portfolios. Most investors consider these options to add diversity into a large portfolio. These alternative debt investments would typically make up 10 to 15 percent of an investment portfolio, and the remaining balance (85–90 percent) would typically be made up of more traditional vehicles such as stocks, bonds, mutual funds, and rental property. This alternative component is important in diversifying because it does not typically move up and down with the economy or the stock and bond markets. In fact, some of these investments perform better when the economy is in recession.

These investments also offer much more personal hands-on control than traditional stocks and bonds. Despite years of experience and careful research, many stock investors lost a lot of money on "Wall Street darlings" such as Lucent, Worldcom, and Enron. In the last recession, the value of "safe" bank stocks was decimated. Even if you did not personally buy these stocks, you may have lost money on them through mutual funds. I am not implying that you should not invest in stocks or funds. A large percentage of my investment portfolio is in the stock market, but there is no doubt that shareholders have *no control* over how a stock is going to perform, and despite all of the stock research that is now available on line, we really have very little insight into how the company is performing. As I write this chapter, two of the world's most respected banks, Wells Fargo and Deutsche Bank, are in the news for corporate scandals, which no investor could have foreseen. These risks are beyond the stockholder's control.

The alternative investments discussed in this book also carry risk, but the risks are more within the control of the investor. The ability to personally manage investment risk is one of the things that has drawn me to these investments, but it isn't for everyone. Are you the type of person who can tolerate risk and is comfortable making decisions?

Clearly, these options are not for everyone. There is no complex math, no calculus or trigonometry required, but each of these investments require a certain level of knowledge and experience. Anyone can learn this stuff, but it may take a few books and some hands-on experience to get you comfortable with them.

There is also a large financial aspect to this. These are not *get-rich-quick* schemes. Most of these investments require a lot of money and a long time frame. Only investors who are financially secure should venture into these waters. And again, most investors should only put 10 or 15 percent of their assets into alternative investments.

Most good things in life come with a price. Since these investments involve more personal control, we have more work to be done. For example, these investments involve haggling with contractors, negotiating a price for note, reviewing a portfolio of credit card debt, or researching property values. This takes some effort. Consider what you are really willing to personally do before you get involved.

My final word of advice is to *be picky*. You don't have to try all of these alternatives. Select the options that appeal to you—if any. Go with your gut and respect your own comfort levels. Then learn more. I have listed books and resources at the end of each chapter, and I am sure there is a mountain of additional information available on the Internet. Read up on the particular subject or subjects that you like. Join LinkedIn discussion groups and build up a solid comfort level before you jump in. Then start small and build up experience.

If none of these alternative options appeal to you, that's fine. They are not for everyone. That is why they are considered "alternative investments." There are plenty of more traditional ways to invest in debt. Just ask your broker about these mainstream options:

TIPS (Treasury Inflation Protection Securities)
REITS
Annuities
Preferred Stocks
Corporate Bonds
Municipal and Treasury bonds
MLP (Master Limited Partnerships)
Mutual funds

Appendix

Due Diligence Checklist—Interior

Address: _____

Systems:
- ✓ Electrical: ☐ Fuses or ☐ Circuit Breakers; Brand of Electrical Box: _____
- ✓ Plumbing: ☐ Water Pressure; ☐ Septic System or ☐ Sewer; ☐ City Water or ☐ Well
- ✓ Heating: ☐ Radiators; ☐ Baseboard; ☐ Hot Air; ☐ Steam; ☐ Gas; ☐ Propane or ☐ Oil
- ✓ Oil Tank: ☐ In Ground; ☐ In Basement or ☐ Outside above-ground;
- ✓ Hot Water Heater: Year and condition: _____
- ✓ Air Conditioning: ☐ Window Units (#____); ☐ Central; Condition: _____

- ✓ Rooms: Bedrooms _____; Bath _____; Dining _____; Living: _____; Other: _____
- ✓ Floor Coverings:
- ✓ Paint/Wall Paper:
- ✓ Ceilings:
- ✓ Basement:
- ✓ Lighting:
- ✓ Fire place:

- ✓ Kitchen: Stove: ☐ Gas or ☐ Electric; ☐ Dishwasher; Overall Condition: _____
- ✓ Cabinets:
- ✓ Countertop:
- ✓ Flooring:
- ✓ Lighting:
- ✓ Appliances:
- ✓ Sink:
- ✓ GFI Outlets:

- ✓ Bathroom:
- ✓ Toilet:
- ✓ Tub / Shower stall:
- ✓ Sink:
- ✓ Mirror:
- ✓ Flooring:
- ✓ Walls:
- ✓ Ceiling:
- ✓ GFI Outlets:

Notes:

Due Diligence Checklist—Exterior

Address: _____

- ✓ Number of Units: ___; □ SFH; □ Up & Down; □ Duplex; □ Apartments; □ Other _____
- ✓ Style: □ Cape; □ Ranch; □ Colonial; □ Tudor; □ Victorian; Other _____
- ✓ Siding: □ Brick; □ Vinyl; □ Alum.; □ Stucco; □ Asbestos; Other _____
- ✓ Windows: #_____; Type: _____; Storm: _____; Condition: _____
- ✓ Garage? □; Attached or Detached? Condition & Materials: _____
- ✓ Driveway? □; Condition & Materials: _____
- ✓ Sidewalks? □; Condition & Materials: _____
- ✓ Roof: Type:_____; Condition: _____; # of layers: _____
- ✓ Chimney: □; Condition & Materials: _____
- ✓ Porch: □; Condition & Materials: _____
- ✓ Fence: □; Condition & Materials: _____
- ✓ Lighting: □; Condition & Type: _____
- ✓ Oil tank: □; Gas Meter: □
- ✓ Pool □; Patio □; Hot Tub □; Car(s) _____
- ✓ Landscaping: _____

Neighborhood:

- ✓ Abandoned houses / Board-ups? □ _____
- ✓ For Sale Listings: _____
- ✓ General Condition and Notes:

SUMMARY NOTES:

About the Author

Michael Pellegrino is an attorney with offices in Denville, New Jersey. His practice has been focused on tax liens and related litigation. He represents large and small tax lien investors and municipalities, as well. Mike has published several articles in professional publications, including a *Law Review* article on the subject of tax liens, and he regularly presents lectures and classes on the subject. He graduated from Rutgers Law School in 1991.

Mike is a former elected councilman in Westwood, New Jersey, and he is the author of a history book about his hometown titled *Westwood,* which was published by Arcadia Press in 2004. Mike also published a book on the history of beer in New Jersey, *Jersey Brew,* in 2009.

Through his law practice, Mike has handled over ten thousand foreclosures, and he has personal experience in each of the investment topics discussed in this book, except life settlements.